Building the Best Faculty

Building the Best Faculty

*Strategies for Hiring and
Supporting New Teachers*

Mary C. Clement

The Scarecrow Press, Inc.
Technomic Books
Lanham, Maryland, and London
2000

SCARECROW PRESS, INC.

Published in the United States of America
by Scarecrow Press, Inc.
4720 Boston Way, Lanham, Maryland 20706
http://www.scarecrowpress.com

4 Pleydell Gardens, Folkestone
Kent CT20 2DN, England

Copyright © 2000 by Mary C. Clement

ISBN 1-56676-735-0 (cloth : alk. paper)
Library of Congress Catalog Card No. 99-63649

☉™ The paper used in this publication meets the minimum requirements of
American National Standard for Information Sciences—Permanence of
Paper for Printed Library Materials, ANSI/NISO Z39.48–1992.
Manufactured in the United States of America.

*Lovingly dedicated to my late mother-in-law,
Virginia P. Lumos, who showed me that the problems I encountered
were really just little inconveniences in my life and could be overcome.
She also taught me that as scary as it may be for a ship to leave its port
and go out onto the ocean, I should remember that there are people
anxiously expecting it on the other side.*

CONTENTS

Chapter 5: The All-Important Interview   23

Chapter 6: Group Interviews   45

Chapter 7: Portfolios, Videos, and Other
Supporting Materials   55

Chapter 8: Final Decisions and Final Negotiations   61

Chapter 9: Problems of Beginning Teachers and the Need for Induction   67

Chapter 10: Orientation   79

Chapter 11: Support Seminars for Newly Hired Teachers   89

I WOULD LIKE to thank Dr. Joseph Eckenrode at Technomic Publishing for his encouragement to develop this book. It simply would not have happened without him.

As always, I want to thank my husband Mark for his continued support. He makes my writing possible by making the computers run and by keeping all the hardware in my life functioning smoothly.

DO YOU REMEMBER your first successful interview in the world of teaching? I certainly do. I was twenty-two years old and wore a home-made blue suit and a polyester flowered blouse (it was the 70s). The principal conducted the interview for about an hour and gave me a short tour of the school. Since I had applied for the position of Spanish teacher, we talked a lot about my junior year of college in Spain, and then the principal said he wanted me to meet the French teacher, since he really didn't know anything about foreign languages. The French teacher told me how important she felt that grammar was and asked me if I felt the same way. One week later the principal called and offered me the job. I accepted and the principal probably never knew that I jumped up and down with excitement at the prospect of securing a job that paid $10,666 dollars a year.

I now know that I fit many statistics as a first-year teacher. I accepted a position that was within one hundred miles of my hometown, as many beginning teachers do. I was asked to teach more of my minor (French) than of my major (Spanish). I did not have a classroom of my own, but had to carry totebags of materials to the French teacher's classroom and to the Latin teacher's classroom. The Latin teacher gave me strict instructions about cleaning the board for her and for keeping the chairs in neat rows. The Latin classroom held eighteen chairs comfortably. The roster for my first Spanish class had twenty-eight names on it. When ten additional chairs were crammed into the Latin room the teacher was not pleased with me. (In educators' terms, I now know this is called "lack of collegial support"!)

One research statistic that I do not fit is that for leaving the profession. Some research tells us that as many as 50% of new teachers leave the profession during the first five years (Haberman, 1995). I stayed in my first teaching job for eight years and left only because I was recruited to teach Spanish at a nearby university.

Once I began working in higher education, I specialized in teacher education, teaching hundreds of seminars for student teachers and beginning teachers. In my work with newly hired teachers, I heard many frustrations from them, such as unmet expectations and how the job "just wasn't what I was led to believe." I then developed an administrators' academy called "Teacher Induction and Mentoring: Providing Ways to Help New Teachers Achieve Success" to try to bridge the gap between what the principal expected from the new hires and the expectations from the teachers about the support they needed. While I had been focusing my work on coaching student teachers on how to find a job, and on how to help new hires survive at jobs, these administrators expressed tremendous concern about the time and effort it took to find good teachers. They revealed many stories of candidates who "looked good on paper," but whose interpersonal skills were so weak that they could not be hired after they interviewed. Some admitted hiring teachers without the exact certification if they felt their basic teaching skills were good, such as hiring a mathematics teacher who was not certified in science to teach science. There was much concern about the maturity level and work commitment exhibited by many new hires.

On several things the administrators always agreed. They did indeed want to hire the best teachers for their faculties. They wanted energetic, enthusiastic teachers who knew their subjects well and who were willing to work hard. They wanted teachers who would project the most positive image to the community and who could "get along well" with the current faculty members. They wanted teachers willing to accept and fulfill extracurricular duties. They wanted team players. Often they expressed the idea that they wanted new faculty who would rejuvenate current faculty. All of these employers also agreed that the entire hiring process from beginning to end was time consuming. Since time is money, the process can be expensive in terms of work hours, and when a teacher leaves at the end of only one year, program continuity may suffer. Parents and students are skeptical of a school where teachers come and go at a high rate of turnover. The majority of administrators also said that they were not taught how to build a new faculty or support their newly hired teachers in their own graduate studies.

This book is designed to help all participants who work in the field of hiring new teachers. Principals, superintendents, staff developers, and personnel officers may use the book to supplement their existing search and hiring practices. New employers will find helpful ideas for developing checklists and evaluation forms. University instructors can find information to help their student teachers conduct job searches, and those who train administrators can use the book as a springboard for discussions and role-plays of how to hire the best new employees.

Hiring new teachers is only the beginning of building the best faculty, however. The dean of the college of education at a university where I used to work always said, "We graduate well-educated teacher education candidates who are ready to go to work in today's classrooms, but they are far from finished products." I have always maintained that the first year of teaching is filled with the most "teachable moments" for the new teacher, and most new teachers agree that they learn the most the first two years "out in the real world." Beginning teachers need to build their confidence, and an environment of "sink or swim" is not conducive to confidence building! Beginning teachers need orientation and support that are ongoing throughout the year. They need to know that they can experiment with new strategies, reach out to parents, and build their teaching repertoire in an environment with a safety net. Supportive administrators and veteran teacher mentors can provide that net. Staff developers in schools can use the chapters of this book devoted to induction and mentoring to refine and improve their programs. Veteran teachers who work as mentors to new teachers will find ideas and guidance. Beginning teachers will find help for starting their careers.

The information shared here has been gathered from experience and from formal and informal research. The names used in the examples, discussion questions, and role-play scenarios are purely fictional. The author recognizes that there is no fool-proof system for hiring new teachers or for implementing staff development that always works, and that the best systems are ones designed locally by each district and building, based on specific needs. However, just as a good wool blazer can be worn in many situations and over many seasons, so too can a good idea for hiring and developing a new faculty member be piloted, used, and refined. It is hoped that these ideas are as useful to you as your favorite wool blazer!

CHAPTER 1

The Need for New Teachers

IT HAS BEEN said that the only constant in education is change, and our school faculties are certainly an example of this. Nationwide, our schools have seen an unprecedented number of retirees in the 1990s and this wave of retirements has come at a time when there is a surge in student enrollment. The organization Recruiting New Teachers, Inc. predicts that "in 1998, more students will be attending American schools than at any other time since 1971" (Haselkorn and Calkins, 1973, p. 6). In addition to surging enrollments, the results of school reform movements include a call for decreased student–teacher ratios. As California began lowering class size, the need for more teachers soared.

MORE STUDENTS, MORE NEEDS

Not only are more students entering the school systems, but there are more students who do not speak English as a native language, and more requiring special assistance for learning disabilities, creating more demand for teachers specializing in those areas. Each year the American Association for Employment in Education (formerly ASCUS) publishes "Teacher Supply and Demand by Field and Region" in their annual *Job Search Handbook for Educators*. Their data indicate considerable teacher shortages in the fields of speech pathology, special education for behavioral disorders, bilingual education, and special education for mentally handicapped (1997). Eighteen other teaching fields are listed as areas with "some shortage." They include five fields of special education, five fields of sciences, mathematics, English as a second language, Spanish, Japanese, audiology, technology education, computer science education, and school psychology (p. 13).

In addition to retirements, growing enrollments, and the need for teachers of high demand fields, there will always be teachers who move to another location and those who simply leave the profession. Much has been written and predicted about a shortage of teachers for America's schools. The report of the National Commission on Teaching and America's Future (1997), *What Matters Most: Teaching for America's Future,* summarizes the shortage as follows: "Over the next decade we will recruit and hire more than two million teachers for America's schools. More than half the teachers who will be teaching ten years from now will be hired during the next decade" (p. 4).

The report also makes a strong case that every student deserves a competent, qualified teacher.

What do all of the facts and figures mean for you, the employer? It means that for some openings, such as a second-grade position in the Midwest, you will probably receive hundreds of applications, all of which are from fully certified teachers. Some of those applicants will be recent twenty-two-year-old graduates, others will be teachers who graduated several years ago and have worked in other positions (banking, secretarial, office management, retailing, etc.) waiting for an elementary position, and still others will be from post-baccalaureate teacher certification programs. Some may have worked as substitutes and aides in order to keep in touch with the profession. Some administrators report that they rarely hire an elementary teacher who hasn't "earned" the position through years of substituting in the district.

The opposite of the above scenario might be one where you need to hire a speech pathologist, a high school physics teacher, or a bilingual teacher. If that is the case, you may have to attend recruitment fairs at out-of-state universities in order to find qualified new teachers. I have known of several school districts that have dropped programs in technical education and automotive sciences because they simply could not find teachers.

Advantages and Disadvantages of Hiring a Substitute

The advantage of hiring a substitute is that he/she may already know much of the school policy and may know many of the students and faculty. They can "hit the ground running." In some districts, substitutes receive staff development and training, and may already be trained in programs specific to your district, such as your classroom management plan and curriculum offerings. You may have had the opportunity to see them teach a lesson while in your building, and may have witnessed their positive interactions with the rest of your staff.

However, selecting a new teacher based only on those available in the pool of substitutes may severely limit your search for the *best* new faculty member. Many outstanding candidates do not choose to do substitute teaching simply because they cannot afford to do so. Substitutes generally do not receive any benefits, making a full-time position as a bank teller more lucrative. Therefore, it is best not to limit searches to just this pool.

A WORD ABOUT POST-BACCALAUREATE TEACHER CERTIFICATION STUDENTS

Post-baccalaureate teacher certification programs have experienced tremendous growth in the 1980s and 1990s. I advised these students for four years at a midwestern university and met with over 200 a year. Those who have chosen to return to college to earn teacher certification after earning an initial bachelor's degree in another field cannot be stereotyped. They include students of all ages, from recent graduates who suddenly do not know what to do with their liberal arts and sciences degree, to retired military personnel in their 50s. Many of my advisees told me that they were recent single parents (both women and men) and saw teaching as their best means of supporting their children while still being able to spend evenings, weekends, and summers with them. Others reported that they had always wanted to be teachers but that their parents would not permit them to major in education. They implied that their parents expected a career with a perceived higher level of professionalism, such as law or medicine. Some post-baccalaureate teacher certification students were, unfortunately, ones who indicated that they were unsuccessful at their chosen jobs, and were unemployed or underemployed. They decided to turn to teaching because "anyone can teach." A few did indeed say that they had decided upon education because they truly loved working with children or because they wanted to make a difference in students' live. Many said that it just took them longer than four years of college to find the right career path.

It is very important to note that the type of post-baccalaureate teacher certification that I worked with was *not* alternative certification, but rather a program that made every student complete all requirements that regular undergraduates in the program would complete. In other universities, post-baccalaureate teacher certification may be an intensive program that leads to a master's in education with initial certification. Some programs exist that require an undergraduate degree in a subject matter field to be completed *before* acceptance into a fifth-year program. Many alternative routes to teacher certification are being developed around the country and some are indeed shortcuts to teaching credentials. As you search for new faculty members and review applications, do not prejudge an application solely on the route that person chose for teacher certification, just as it is hoped that you do not judge applicants only on their college of graduation. As an employer, you need to be aware of the different routes that lead to teacher certification, but also to be aware that someone's life experiences may help them to be a more mature, well-rounded teacher. Because there can be so many variables in selecting a newly hired teacher, it is even more important that you envision the job that you need done in your school, and create objective and judicious procedures for looking at all candidates.

WHY SPEND SO MUCH EFFORT IN HIRING THE BEST?

I hope that you are not even asking this question, but, if some teachers can be found for "a dime a dozen," why should you spend so much time searching and developing them as faculty? The answer is quality. The answer is your responsibility to the community in which you serve as an administrator. The answer is that every child deserves the best teacher, because it is not easy to get a good education and get ahead in today's world. Georgia educator Martha Berry said, "We walk into tomorrow on the lives of our youth." The comfort of your retirement depends upon the job skills of the students in your school now, because it takes employed workers to keep retirement funds solvent.

The pragmatic answer to this question is that spending time up front in your search and in the initial year of the teacher's employment will save you much time down the road. Parents will not be phoning you to complain about a successful teacher who is thriving in the classroom. School board members will not be calling special sessions of the board to dismiss teachers who are achieving the desired goals. Quite frankly, if you want to move up the ladder of administration, hiring the best and brightest and supporting them to success will also help you to succeed. If this has not convinced you to read on, then nothing will!

KEY POINTS

(1) Growing student enrollments, teacher retirements, and the increased demand for specialty areas of teaching create a continual need for new teachers.

(2) Administrators who find and retain the best new teachers will reap the rewards of a quality teaching faculty.

(3) Increased student achievement and positive public relations with the community should result from a quality school faculty.

CHAPTER 2

Envisioning and Defining the New Position

GOALS AND OBJECTIVES

In Education 101 classes we were all taught never to plan a lesson without first defining our goals and objectives. Whenever an opening occurs at your school, remember to do just that. The defining of goals and objectives can also be called envisioning the new position. Sometimes the goal of getting a new teacher hired is entirely too vague—we want someone who can "do the job," "inspire the kids," or worse yet, "just control the kids"! On the other hand, it would be trite to make a job description that read like a behavioral objective. Wanted: By June 1, with the minimum of materials and cost to the district, the new teacher will have taught reading, writing, mathematics, social studies, science, and multiculturalism to thirty-seven third-graders with 85% accuracy, as determined by the mandated goals achievement test. The teacher will also prevent headlice in at least 95% of the students and supervise a daily playground period where fewer than 5% of students will need to visit the school nurse.

Just because Mr. Gaddis has taught six classes of general United States history for the last fourteen years, has sponsored the student council, and served as the assistant track coach, does that necessarily mean that the new hire must do that exact assignment? If a new teacher is spending hours and hours of time with the student council and the track team, will he/she have time to become established in the classroom?

A similar question to ask involves the teacher's grade-level preference. If a teacher interviews and indicates that he/she really wants to teach first-graders, how happy will that teacher be if the first two years they are assigned only fifth-graders? If that teacher feels threatened by the older students, what will happen to classroom management?

As you envision the new teaching position at your school, try to develop that position with the goal of teacher success. What factors will contribute to the success of a newly hired teacher in the position? Leslie Huling-Austin's research (1989b) indicated that the "placement of the first-year teacher may well be the most influential variable related to first year teaching success" (p. 16). Factors that will contribute to a positive teaching assignment include (Huling-Austin, 1989b):

(*1*) Being assigned in an area that matches the candidate's background and training
(*2*) Having limited teaching preparations
(*3*) Not having time-consuming and demanding extracurricular responsibilities
(*4*) Not working with remedial and/or unmotivated students
(*5*) Having one's own classroom

BEGINNING TEACHERS HAVE RELATED THE FOLLOWING TRUE STORIES

Lisa, a recent graduate, was hired to teach six fifty-minute classes a day in her new position as a high school English teacher. Each class was relatively large, between twenty-seven and thirty-two students. At the first faculty meeting a veteran pulled her aside and informed her that she was hired to replace two retired teachers, each of whom had taught five small classes a day. Since ten small classes taught by two veteran teachers had been reduced to six large classes taught by a new teacher, the district saved almost sixty thousand dollars in salaries. In addition, Lisa had agreed to sponsor the scholastic bowl team and to coach the junior varsity girls' softball team to make herself even more employable. What do you think that Lisa's stress level was like that first year? How effective was she in working with her six classes, all of whom included a diverse level of learners? I happen to know that because of her strong work ethic and commitment to succeeding, Lisa survived two years at this school in order to get a recommendation that wouldn't look bad on a resumé. However, she left after two years to pursue an advanced degree, with hopes of teaching at the college level or in a private school. In her own words, "I want to teach somewhere where they respect the students enough not to throw them all together in big classes, and where they respect the teachers enough not to give them the heaviest possible work loads."

Kathy, a speech communication-theater major, was hired to teach general English at a small rural high school, where she could also sponsor the spring play. She assumed that she knew what general English was, but was shocked to learn that in all five of her junior and senior classes there were students with reading levels of third to eighth grade, and that most of the students had already failed at least one English class. While the students had not been diagnosed as special education students, and therefore could not receive the services from the special education department, Kathy knew enough from her one college class about learning disorders to realize that over half of her students had learning disabilities and/or could have been classified as having behavior disorders. Kathy perceived by November that this was not how she wanted to earn a living, and that this position was not going to help build her career. She wrote a letter to resign at the end of the first semester, but was encouraged enough by her principal to stay until the end of the school year. After taking some time off to get her English certification, she returned to teaching later at a different school. (She reported that her marriage suffered tremendously from job-related stress, and that she used every sick day she had that year.)

How can situations like those of Lisa and Kathy be avoided? When a new position occurs, define or redefine the position so that it can be a successful one. If many students potentially belong in special education, make sure that the paperwork is done so that those students can receive special help and teachers trained to deal with their needs. Read the research about class size and be prepared to go to the board of education requesting more, not fewer, teachers for positions that arise.

Write a job description that is accurate in tone. Advertise for a teacher of remedial English if that is indeed where the opening has occurred. If you do need a cafeteria supervisor, a coach, or an activities sponsor, then include that in the original job description so that all applicants know about the extra duties up front. Some new teachers thrive on extra duties and have the boundless energy required to complete those duties. The most important thing about the job description is that it reflect your expectations accurately. A new teacher who has been trained to work with behavior disordered students, who had experiences with these students in student teaching, and who feels that is part of his/her commitment to teaching can do an excellent job with those students. In fact, they might not feel comfortable teaching advanced placement students who challenge the teacher in other ways. The success depends upon the match of teacher and job, and the match begins with a clear definition of the position.

POSSIBLE SCENARIOS AND QUESTIONS FOR DISCUSSION

(1) Beginning teachers bemoan the fact that they traditionally have to deal with the heaviest work loads, the worst students, and the smallest classrooms. How can equitable assignments be made, such that this does not occur?

(2) When one teacher leaves, there may be others who want the classroom that he/she had, leaving the smallest, most remote classroom for the newly hired teacher. How can you solve this dilemma, making both veteran and new teachers satisfied?

(3) With growing enrollments, you may not have a classroom for the newly hired teacher. What can you do to facilitate this teacher's work and give him/her the most support without a classroom?

(4) Discuss the role of the teachers' union in determining class size and number of preparations that a teacher may be assigned. What role, if any, do the unions in your area take in new teacher assignments, such as those assignments based on seniority?

(5) Student teachers are trained to ask, "Why has this position become open?" If you were asked this question by Lisa (from the scenario in this chapter), how would you respond?

KEY POINTS

(1) Create teaching positions that are realistic and "doable" by the new faculty member.

(2) The best time to realign a faculty position is before the position is advertised.

CHAPTER 3

Advertising and Recruiting

I HEARD A SPEAKER use the phrase "the litigious 90s" earlier this year as she described the need for teachers to be ever vigilant in their recordkeeping to avoid lawsuits and litigation. I will use this same not-so-subtle warning to all employers as they begin advertising and recruiting new teachers. Many school districts have written policies regarding how and when positions will be advertised. The teachers' union may have helped write the policy and may have negotiated it as part of their districtwide contract. First and foremost, advertise the position openings as outlined by your district policy. If your district does not have a formal policy, you may want to develop a policy, working with your teachers to do so. It is not uncommon for a policy to include the advertisement of a position internally first, before the job description is sent to a newspaper or university placement service. You will want to advertise positions throughout your district anyway. There may be a strong candidate within the district who thrives on changing assignments or on changing grade levels. You may have internal candidates who took a job teaching more of their minor than of their major in order to work in your district, and they may be thrilled at the prospect of finally getting to teach their strongest area.

After internal advertising, do not hesitate to use the most common source in the world—newspaper want ads. Depending upon your budgetary constraints, you will want to consider several newspapers, especially Sunday editions, which typically have the largest number of job advertisements. Listing in both the city and college newspaper may prove rewarding. Some newspapers now list their classified advertisements on their website, so always inquire if the listing in the paper will be listed online as well. For an example of online classified ads for educators from a newspaper, check out www.atlantaclassifieds.com/employ.htm on the World Wide Web.

THE COLLEGE CAREER CENTER

The career center or placement office of a college can provide invaluable help as you advertise for new faculty. Most publish a bulletin of job openings where you can advertise—almost always for free. Many centers now put their bulletins on their homepage, providing more extensive advertising for you. Some centers also have databases of their current graduates, so you can receive a listing of students with the certification that you seek. You can mail the potential candidates a form letter about your school, informing them of the opening and inviting them to apply. If you are searching for a candidate in a high-demand field, or if you live in an area with teacher shortages, you may need to do this type of recruitment by mail. Again, most college students not only have e-mail, but use it all the time. You can send one e-mail message to an unlimited number of potential candidates at as many universities as you choose by requesting e-mail addresses of candidates listed in the placement centers' database. When candidates register with their placement office, they have given the office their permission to put their name, address, and areas of certification on this type of list. The same is true of the e-mail address. Discuss the issue of right to privacy with the center if you have any questions.

The career center/placement office can do even more to help you. Find out if they hold employment fairs and, if so, participate in those fairs. By setting up a booth at the job fair you will be able to meet a large number of candidates in a short amount of time. Gather as many resumés as possible during the fair, then evaluate them back in your office to decide which candidates to interview. The placement center will often set up a time for you to recruit on their campus even if they are not sponsoring a job fair. I have known career center directors who will advertise your interview times in advance, provide you with an interview room for the day, and even give you a student worker to run your errands and be your secretary while interviewing candidates. Some may even buy you lunch! Remember that career centers exist to help the college's students find jobs, and that they must prove their effectiveness every year in order to retain their funding. They are motivated to help you. Work with several colleges and universities, both public and private, to broaden the base of your pool of potential new teachers. Remember that some of the midwestern universities are still producing many more teachers than their state markets demand, and are actually "exporting" teachers to other states after graduation.

What *can't* the university career placement center do for you? They cannot sort candidates and give you a short list of the "best" candidates or a list of only minority candidates. The days of county superintendents calling a college and requesting that they send their best majors out for an interview are over.

Other Sources for Job Fairs and Advertising

The Job Search Handbook for Educators, published by the American Association for Employment in Education, was cited in Chapter 1; it is also an excellent source for finding out about national job fairs and a good place to advertise your district. The AAEE can be contacted at 820 Davis Street, Suite 222, Evanston, IL 60201–4445, phone 847–864–1999.

The *Careers in Teaching Handbook* (1993, available by calling 1–800–45–TEACH) lists multiple sources of online databases. They include:

- Educators OnLine, 2011 Crystal Drive, Suite 813, Arlington, VA 22202; 800–374–8322
- Connexion, 202 Carnegie Center, PO Box 2123, Princeton, NJ 08543; 800–338–3282
- KiNexus National Data Center, 640 N. Lasalle, Suite 560, Chicago, IL 60610; 800–828–0422

Again, the career services office of a university may have even more appropriate sources for online job advertising.

ADVERTISING THE POSITION

I had originally planned to call this chapter "Truth in Advertising" because I feel so strongly that all employers must be forthright in their advertisements of position openings. Everything from the previous chapter regarding definition of the position should be included in the advertisement of the position. If you are searching for a junior high Spanish teacher who can coach the girls' golf team and also sponsor the high school play, then advertise for that. Share as much about the defined position as you can in the advertising process. It may also prove very worthwhile to list the base salary for a position in the district. After all, what are the most pressing questions for most candidates? They are "What is the assignment?" and "How much will I earn?" While many graduates do become educators because it is a way to help young people, teaching is a way to earn a living, and very few teachers can afford to do the job without the salary. The more information that is covered up front and in a forthright manner, the more smoothly the rest of the interview and induction process will go. Problems arise when expectations are not met. When expectations are met, teachers experience much higher levels of satisfaction.

Your advertisement should include

(*1*) The description of the position and certifications necessary to be considered

(*2*) The last date that complete applications will be accepted for consideration

(*3*) The beginning date of employment and the date by which the candidate must prove certification

(*4*) A list of all paperwork needed for consideration: a cover letter, resumé, and how many letters of application are required

(*5*) Statement of any extracurricular duties included

(*6*) Statement of base pay

(*7*) District's statement related to equal consideration or affirmative action hiring practices

(*8*) Statement of where application materials should be sent and statement of how candidates should follow up on the application process

Wanted: Columbia Middle School in the heart of Springfield seeks a full-time teacher of social sciences and language arts to teach two sixth-grade language arts classes, two seventh-grade language arts classes, and two eighth-grade classes of state and national government. Position start date is August 15. Candidate must provide proof of certification in middle school language arts and social science (Type 42 certificate with SS and LA endorsements) at time of interview or no later that July 30. The applicant will also be asked to serve as an assistant in preparing seventh-graders for the state academic bowl and for coaching either seventh-grade cheerleaders or eighth-grade boys basketball. The base salary for the next school year is $24,678. and each coaching or academic sponsorship pays 3.6% of base salary. For full consideration please send a cover letter, resumé, three letters of recommendation, and official transcripts to Ms. Harriett Tyler, Columbia Middle School, 200 East 14th Street, Springfield, Anystate, Zip code. Upon receipt of your materials, an application will be mailed to you. The application and all materials must be received by the school no later than May 20. Requests for applications may be made by calling 211–111–3333 between 8 A.M.

and 4 P.M. Materials may be dropped off at the Middle School, but applicant should not expect to meet with anyone involved in the hiring process when leaving materials. Columbia Middle School is an equal opportunity employer.

QUESTIONS FOR FURTHER DISCUSSION

(*1*) Much has been discussed about use of the internet for advertising and recruitment of teachers. How useful do you find online resources for advertising in your area? Is e-mail a viable alternative for reaching candidates to set up their interviews, and so on?

(*2*) How do you handle receiving hundreds of applications for a position that was only advertised locally? If you know that a position will be filled internally, should you advertise in any other sources?

(*3*) Candidates may send letters and resumés to your district when no openings have occurred and none are expected. What do you do with these materials? Do you respond with a form letter? How long do you keep these unsolicited materials?

KEY POINTS

(*1*) Take advantage of college career centers whenever possible.

(*2*) Remember "truth in advertising" when describing a position opening.

(*3*) Take advantage of the technology of online advertising.

CHAPTER 4

Reviewing and Evaluating the Paperwork

THE FIRST SORT—IS THE CANDIDATE CERTIFIED OR NOT?

The question, "Is the candidate certified," is a yes/no question. Yet, the answer to this question is often "almost." The certification paperwork for a new graduate, or for a returning student who has just completed post-baccalaureate certification, may take several weeks for the university and state agency to process. Students who complete programs in the spring semester can get their paperwork done before the start of fall classes at your school. Those who student teach in the spring, but who still must complete requirements during summer school may not have their certification by the start of your school year. A student's resumé or cover letter should state clearly if they have received certification, or if they have applied and it is expected. To cover your own hiring needs, new teachers hired with certification pending should be told in writing that their hiring is dependent upon receipt of certification by a certain date. Some candidates now include a photocopy of their teaching certificate in their application materials. If you require this, you must include that specification in your advertisement.

Candidates who are certified to teach in the grade and field of the position, or who have completed their program of study and are awaiting their paperwork, are the only ones who should be considered for evaluation for an interview. Hiring noncertified teachers creates one problem after another for you and the teacher. The debate over "certified" versus "qualified" will rage forever, but the truth is that the state teaching certification is the closest standardized measure that exists for evaluating "qualified" to teach. State standards have become increasingly more rigorous, as have university requirements. If the university has met the standards of the National Council for Accreditation of Teacher Education (NCATE), then their programs have passed even more evaluations.

Some administrators may argue that they simply could not find any candidates with the required certifications for the advertised position. What can be done if this is the case? There are many options, including:

(*1*) Redefine the position. The principal of a small school needed a teacher for English and Spanish because of a retirement. No candidates with dual certification applied. Redefining the position as two part-time ones could solve the problem.

(*2*) Begin the search earlier and make the search broader. If you know in advance of an opening for the upcoming year, begin the recruitment process by attending MANY job fairs. It is not unreasonable to expect an employer to attend a dozen job fairs, both in state and out of state, and to advertise in thirty to forty university bulletins. Online advertising may net an even larger audience. This is time-consuming and travel expenses add to the cost of recruitment, so the budget will have to be determined at least a year in advance. Plan ahead.

(*3*) Begin continual planning for hiring new faculty and "grow your own." Accepting more student teachers from multiple universities is one way to recruit new graduates to your district. Begin discussions with the director of field experiences and/or dean of the college of education at nearby universities and those that are out of state. If in-state universities are not producing the number of graduates needed in the shortage areas, let them know and let your state legislators know. Students and parents continue to ask the career counselors about the best fields for employment.

(*4*) Develop joint partnerships with community colleges and universities. Community colleges train teachers' aides, some of whom could transfer to universities to finish their certification if enough advisement and support were provided them (Clement, 1991).

REVIEW AND EVALUATION OF THE PAPERWORK

Mountains of paperwork may appear in your office after you have advertised the vacant positions. Begin dealing with the paperwork by creating a file for each candidate. Your support staff should file each piece of paperwork as it arrives, marking on the front of the file the date of arrival. Before reading any candidate's file, you should have established criteria for evaluating all files (see Figure 1). Should you consider an incomplete candidate file? Teachers need to be able to meet deadlines, and being able to get all relevant paperwork to your office

Candidate's name:
Position sought:

Disagree.....Disagree somewhat.....Average.....Agree somewhat.....Agree completely
   1   2   3   4   5

Cover letter

Content is clearly expressed	1....2....3....4....5
Presentation is neat, well typed, no typos	1....2....3....4....5
Notes:	

Resumé

Candidate's work experience is appropriate	1....2....3....4....5
Candidate's education is appropriate	1....2....3....4....5
Candidate has awards, activities, professional memberships or other related experiences	1....2....3....4....5
Resumé presentation is clear, easy to read, no typos	1....2....3....4....5
Notes:	

Letters of recommendation

Letters recommended candidate strongly	1....2....3....4....5
Letters indicated examples of successful teaching experience	1....2....3....4....5
Letters indicated many strengths, such as energy, enthusiasm, ability to work with others	1....2....3....4....5
Letters showed no areas of concern	1....2....3....4....5
Notes:	

Transcripts

Students grade point average is _____
Notes:

Total points from this evaluation _____
Total possible   50 plus grade point

Using this form:

This form is quite simplistic, but you see the idea behind trying to sort and quantify the vast amounts of material coming into your office when there is a job opening. You will want forms that are short and simple to use if you are evaluating 87 sets of applications, or 187! While the evaluation is still subjective, you can make it more objective with your own criteria, such as rating all student teachers a "3" for experience, those with one or two years a "4," and those with more than three years a "5" if you are searching for an experienced teacher. Try this form as a starting point and create your own.

Figure 1 Pre-interview evaluation of paperwork.

on time in the application process may be the first indicator of how a candidate will turn in paperwork as a teacher. Deems (1994) says, "The single best predictor of future job performance is past job behavior" (p. 15).

THE COVER LETTER

The cover letter is the candidate's best shot at impressing you and getting you to read the supporting materials. It should be clearly written, well typed, and without misspelled words. The signature should be legible. The content of the letter should be clear and should hold your interest, pointing out that this candidate has some experience that will set him/her apart from the competition. While a little humor can be a good thing, there should be absolutely no sarcasm or jokes in the letter. The cover letter must sell you on this candidate, and it is also a sample of the types of letters that the candidate will be capable of writing to parents once he/she becomes a teacher. (See Figure 1 for a checklist to evaluate all the pre-interview paperwork.)

THE RESUMÉ

Every college and university offers seminars on how to write a resumé. Many times the teacher education student must write a resumé as an assignment in a pre-student teaching class. Many students buy how-to books such as Parker's (1989) *The Damn Good Resume Guide*. With all the time and energy spent on resumé writing, resumés should look really good—both in presentation and in content. The resumé should outline educational experience, work experience in education and in other fields, relevant professional awards, committees, and memberships. As recently as the 1970s, candidates were still putting personal information, such as marital status, on their resumés, but that is not done anymore. (The next chapter will address candidates' civil rights and what can and cannot be addressed during the interviewing process, including marital status.) The resumé may cover types of certifications held, and, in essence, should make a strong case for you to hire the candidate. Resumés on neon-colored paper or delivered via special express in a decorated envelope are generally not well received. Some employers feel that the candidate who goes overboard on presentation may be trying to compensate for lack of real background and experience in the resumé.

THE LETTERS OF RECOMMENDATION

All candidates choose writers of their letters who will say "nice things." In evaluating letters you need to learn to read between the lines and look for areas of concern (red flags). As a student teaching supervisor, I have written many letters of recommendation. In fact, NOT having a letter from a new graduate's university supervisor or the classroom co-operating/supervisory teacher may be such a red flag for concern. When I wrote letters for strong candidates, my letters stated that the candidate was strong, and that they were indeed ready for their first classroom. I usually ended such a letter by stating that I recommended the candidate wholeheartedly. If the student teacher was not a strong candidate, my letter stated that the candidate had completed student teaching for the required number of weeks. I generally ended these letters by urging the reader to contact the student and request permission to discuss the student teaching experience with the classroom supervisory teacher. In a few cases, if a student teacher was exceptionally weak, I simply told the student that I felt that someone else should write them a letter of recommendation. My approach to writing letters for student teachers is a fairly common one.

A strong letter of recommendation may include one or two vignettes of successful teaching, such as describing how the candidate worked diligently at tutoring or how they developed lesson plans that kept students actively involved. Good letters of recommendation discuss the teacher's enthusiasm, energy, and desire to do a superior job. They may include a brief reference to the teacher's hobby or special interest that he/she brought into the classroom for an enrichment project. If you want to hire dynamic teachers who work well in groups, look for specific examples in their letters of reference. Another strong recommendation is one where the writer ranks the candidate highly compared to others with whom they have worked.

A Word of Warning About Letters of Reference

Some people still do not write glowing words about teachers. Some supervisors, either university or practicing principals, always end letters by saying that the candidate has room for improvement. This can be a cause for concern, since saying there is room for improvement may be one administrator's way of saying "don't hire this candidate" or another administrator's way of ending letters about young teachers in general—even excellent ones. Hopefully, the other letters will contain clues that help you to decide for yourself.

The candidate may or may not know what the writers of letters of recommendation have written. In the past, letters were often kept secret from the candidates, but this is rarely the case today. If a candidate's letters come from the placement office of the university, the candidate retains the option of an open or closed file, and most offices recommend the open file where a candidate may read all letters and then decide which ones he/she wants to be forwarded. While a few universities still put a copy of the classroom teacher's evaluation of a student teacher in his/her file, many choose not to do this, believing that this evaluation, like a test score, is the right of the student to keep private.

Having received a letter of recommendation does not automatically give the employer the right to call that writer for further information about the candidate. The right to contact recommendation writers must be secured from the candidate. Candidates may state in their cover letter that the writers of their letters may be contacted for further information. University placement offices may get the candidate's permission for this when the candidate activates a file. If this is the case the cover letter from the university will clearly state it.

TRANSCRIPTS

You will want to set your own evaluation of transcripts and grades. Do grades reflect the student's work ethic? Do grades reflect the student's ability to get up in the morning and get to class on time? Do poor grades as a freshman reflect anything other than the difficulty in adjusting to the university? The process of grading remains one of the the most debated topics in education. No one is going to hire solely on the basis of a grade point average, but the transcripts may be one indicator to help you as you evaluate a candidate.

YOUR DISTRICT'S APPLICATION

In addition to the standard paperwork submitted by applicants, your district may create its own application. This application may help you to further standardize applicants' qualifications. Basic information needed on the application would include:

(*1*) Name, address, phone, e-mail address

(*2*) Position sought

(*3*) Certifications held

(*4*) Available start date

(*5*) Names, addresses, phones, and e-mail addresses of references that the employer may contact

(*6*) Names and dates of college attendance

(*7*) Years of experience and names of employers for teaching and other work

(*8*) Interest and background in extracurricular coaching and sponsorships

(*9*) Statement of philosophy of education or an example of applicant's most positive teaching experience

(*10*) Attach a sample lesson plan, unit plan, or test

Some employers request that the candidate *write* parts of the application so that they have a sample of handwriting. If you want this to be part of your evaluation, then tell the applicant so in the instructions of the application.

The application should provide you with more information about the candidate, and do so in an organized manner for easy comparison to other candidates. The comparison of candidates needs to be objective, and as quantifiable as possible. For this reason, many employers create checklists and rating sheets to assist them in the process of reading the paperwork. The sample worksheet in Figure 1 are designed to help you create ones specific to your district's position openings. If more than one person reviews the initial paperwork, ratings can be easily tallied to give a committee an overview of rankings. It is wise to print a disclaimer on any review sheets that they are not intended for use as the determining factor in who will be interviewed and hired. Determine well in advance who will see these sheets and what the specific use will be. Also determine in advance if the sheets will be placed in the candidates' files or if they will be used for general screening purposes and then destroyed.

QUESTIONS

(*1*) Discuss this statement, "If you want a good teacher, hire a good student." Then discuss, "If you want a good teacher, hire a student with good grades."

(*2*) Should handwriting samples be considered for employment as a teacher? (It can be argued that teachers will do a lot of writing and if students can't read the teacher's writing, the learning process will be slowed. However, it can also be argued that with today's technologies, students will never see the teacher's handwriting, just word processing.)

KEY POINTS

(*1*) Answer the question, "Is the candidate certified?" and search broadly for certified candidates.

(*2*) Review cover letters and resumés remembering that they should be best examples of the candidate's written communication.

(*3*) Letters of reference may vary for new graduates. Know the writer and learn to "read between the lines."

(*4*) Create an application and an evaluation instrument that help you quantify the qualifications of applicants.

CHAPTER 5

The All-Important Interview

IT HAS BEEN said over and again, "You only get one chance to make a good first impression." The candidate will be trying to make a good impression, and the impression that you receive from this person will be similar to the one that parents, other teachers, administrators, and school board members get. A candidate who appears in casual dress for an interview will probably dress that way for parent conference night. What impression will this make on the parents in attendance? Students take note of everything that their teacher does, and a teacher with a vague expression and inaudible voice will not be well received by students. Both students and parents want teachers who appear to "have it all together." Back in the 1980s some of the literature about teaching also called the effective teacher one with "with-itness." While the purpose of the interview is to assess the candidate's ability to do the job of classroom teacher, you will also get a sense of the candidate's interpersonal communication skills, social skills, and their "with-itness" from the interview.

HOW TEACHERS ARE INTERVIEWED

Eighty-four percent of newly hired teachers reported that they were interviewed by principals (Anthony and Head, 1991). Fifty-four percent reported being interviewed by a district-level personnel officer, 33% by a superintendent, and 26% by assistant principals and committees (Anthony and Head, 1991). Obviously, some candidates are interviewed more than once, and by more than one person. This chapter is designed to help you as you interview one-on-one with candidates, assessing their previous work experience by asking pertinent questions about teaching. The following chapter will deal with group interviews. A checklist/evaluation of potential questions is presented at the end of the chapter. The checklist is designed to be a starting point for you to build your own set of relevant questions.

EXTENDING THE INVITATION FOR AN INTERVIEW

How many candidates should you interview? This will depend upon the type of position that is open, your district's geographic location, the number of applicants, your available time, and other variables. You are looking for the right match—someone who has the skills, the certification, the experience, and the desire to teach in your school district. You need someone who CAN do the job and someone who is ready to do the job.

When calling applicants to invite them for an interview, let them know the specifics of the interview. These include:

- whether the candidate is still available and still interested in position
- when the interview will take place
- where it will take place
- who will be conducting the interview
- what type of interview it will be (one-on-one, committee, principal and department chair, etc.)
- whether or not the interview will be recorded, and if so, for whom
- approximate length of interview
- any special materials required at the time of the interview, such as proof of citizenship/eligibility to work, further documentation of teaching certificate, and so on.

Whenever possible, try to avoid leaving messages with parents, children, or roommates.

You may choose to call applicants and conduct a telephone interview before inviting the candidate to your school. This is done routinely by universities recruiting new professors from out of state. Create a guideline for your telephone interviews that is similar to the guideline for in-person interviews. Always let the candidate know if your call is informational or an actual telephone interview.

SCENARIO FOR DISCUSSION

As an employer, you have just called a college senior to invite him/her for an interview. The candidate is not home and this is the message on his/her answering machine, "Hi! This is Terry. I can't come to the phone right now, but if you have beer, I'll arrange the party. If you want a date, I'm always free. Leave your number and let's party!" How, if at all, are you influenced by this message?

YOUR QUESTIONS

It is a good idea for you to ask the same list of questions to each candidate. It not only keeps you organized, but makes it easier for you to compare candidates' responses. You may keep the questions on paper in front of you, telling the candidate that you have developed a set of questions and that each question will be asked of every candidate. If you are taking notes or completing an evaluation during the interview, you should inform the candidate. Employers may tape- or video record interviews, but candidates must be made aware of the recording. It is best to tell them of the recording when they are invited to interview, not just when they arrive for the interview. As an employer you may review a videotaped interview at your convenience to evaluate the interview. You may also send the tape to other teachers or administrators for review, provided the candidate has been informed and has given permission for this. Districts using videotaped interviews have developed policies for correct use of the tapes, and when a candidate is invited to interview every step of the policy is outlined during the invitation and again before the interview begins.

You may want your questions on your laptop computer for reference, scrolling through them as the interview progresses. You may be able to enter your evaluation numbers into the computer very discreetly, making the interview process even smoother. Technology should enhance your work, not slow it down! Each interviewer will develop his/her own style for assessing and evaluating the interview. Since I have observed student teachers for several years, I like to write short notes as I work with someone, so that we may have a productive conference later. In an interview situation, I would keep my list of questions on my desk, write down key words from the candidate's responses, and then complete a numerical evaluation of those responses immediately after the candidate left. I always like to use simple numerical scales, such as 1 to 5. Would I hire the person with the highest total number of points? Not necessarily, but I would use the evaluation to remind myself of candidates' answers and to review the candidates.

It is obvious that yes/no answers will not be of much help to you in the interview process. You want to design and ask open-ended questions that ask for specific examples that you can evaluate (Deems, 1994). By focusing and grouping your questions on the different aspects of teaching, such as strategies, classroom management, and communicating with parents, you should be able to get an idea about whether the candidate can talk about teaching. Teaching and talking about how to teach are still two different entities, but someone who can't even talk about how to plan a lesson or how to implement an effective classroom management plan, won't be able to do those things. Much of teaching consists of presenting new material and explaining information to students. An interviewee who can thoroughly explain a grading scale to you can also explain it to students and parents.

WHAT YOU CANNOT ASK

You may not ask any discriminatory questions. Your questions must be in regard to bona fide occupational qualifications. Federal legislation prohibits you from asking about age, sex, marital status, ethnic origin, religious preference, sexual preference, and disabilities (Deems, 1994; Krannich and Krannich, 1997). In addition, some states prohibit questions about smoking.

In addition to not asking about age, sex, marital status, ethnic origin, religious preference, sexual preference, disabilities, and smoking directly, you may not ask questions that are phrased indirectly at getting at the same topics. For example, noticing someone's last name, you cannot ask the origin of their name. You cannot ask about number of children or about child care, as that relates to marital status. Asking about a striking piece of jewelry may be discriminatory, as it may be asking about a piece of jewelry with religious significance, or with marital significance (not everyone wears their wedding band on the same finger).

When I served on interview committees at the university level, I kept a list of the topics that could not be discussed in front of me during the interview. In fact, our committees gave all interviewers and candidates the list for interviews. It helps as a reminder. It is so easy to forget and to ask someone the wrong question. Questions such as, "Where are you from originally?" and "How many children do you have?," are considered small talk or icebreakers by some people at a dinner party or in the dentist's waiting room. These are not icebreakers in the interview, but illegal questions.

FIRST IMPRESSIONS

The candidate should be appropriately dressed. This generally means a clean, pressed suit with dress shoes. Jewelry on men or women should not be outlandish, and hair should be clean and groomed. The candidate should arrive on time, or even a little early. The candidate should be absolutely pleasant and formal when introducing himself/herself to secretaries and support staff, as well as to the interviewer. A firm handshake and the ability to smile and make eye contact are very important. The candidate may be nervous, and a little nervousness is to be expected. (See Figure 2 for an interview checklist/evaluation form.)

SCENARIOS FOR DISCUSSION

(1) While walking through the hall before lunch, the principal sees a young man in shorts and a tee shirt peering into classroom doors. The principal approaches the man and asks him why he is in the building. (There is a large sign at all entrances stating that visitors must register in the office, and this visitor has not done so.) The young man replies that he is Thomas Scott, and that he has a job interview with the principal at 2 P.M. He says that he wanted to "check out" the school and "get a feel" for the learning environment before his interview. As the principal, what is your reaction to Thomas' unannounced visit? Will it influence your decision to hire him?

(2) Everyone's opinion of fashion is different. Discuss what you might consider outlandish or totally inappropriate hair, dress, or jewelry. If a candidate wears tennis shoes and white socks with a very appropriate suit, would that influence your appraisal of "appropriate dress?" (Remember, you can't ask about the tennis shoes, because that can be considered a discriminatory question, related to disabilities. Besides, it can be argued that you want teachers who wear comfortable shoes because teachers need to be on their feet, not seated at their desks.)

(3) Susan has applied for a position teaching preschool at your elementary school. She arrives for the interview wearing knee-length denim walking shorts and a paint-splattered white cotton shirt. Almost immediately she explains that she chose this outfit because this is typical of what she wears to work. She believes that when working with three- and four-year-olds the teacher must be actively involved and that she always is. How will you evaluate her on the category of "appropriate dress"?

Candidate's name:
Position sought:

Weak......Below Average......Average......Fairly Strong......Very Strong
   1   2   3   4   5

Overall impression

(1) Appropriate dress   1....2....3....4....5
(2) Arrived on time   1....2....3....4....5
(3) First impression (handshake, eye contact, etc.)   1....2....3....4....5

Notes:

Icebreaker questions (not necessarily for evaluation)

(1) Tell me about yourself
(2) What would you like to tell me that is not on your resumé?
(3) You have indicated that you have been involved with_____.
    Could you tell me about that?
(4) What made you choose teaching as your profession?

Notes:

Knowledge of teaching/subjects

(1) What should the curriculum be for this grade/subject area?   1....2....3....4....5
(2) How will you design unit plans for your teaching?   1....2....3....4....5
(3) How do you plan lessons? (Which model of lesson plan do you
    use? What do your plans look like?)   1....2....3....4....5
(4) Which models of teaching do you use?   1....2....3....4....5
(5) Which teaching strategies are successful with this age student?   1....2....3....4....5
(6) How do you begin a lesson/class?   1....2....3....4....5
(7) Is group work appropriate for your class? If so, when?   1....2....3....4....5
(8) What is a typical homework assignment for this class?   1....2....3....4....5
(9) What are some good techniques for ending class?   1....2....3....4....5
(10) Explain your preferred ways of grading.   1....2....3....4....5
(11) How can you meet individual academic needs of students—those
    who excel and those who need extra help?   1....2....3....4....5
(12) What are some characteristics of truly effective teachers?   1....2....3....4....5

Notes:

Classroom management

(1) With which classroom management writers or theorists are you
    familiar?   1....2....3....4....5
(2) How would you create and implement a classroom management
    plan?   1....2....3....4....5
(3) What rewards and consequences are appropriate for your students? 1....2....3....4....5
(4) How will you communicate your classroom management plan to
    students and parents?   1....2....3....4....5
(5) Candidate's past experience with successful classroom
    management.   1....2....3....4....5

Figure 2 Interview checklist/evaluation.

(*6*) Response to a hypothetical situation. (What would you do if . . .)   1....2....3....4....5

Notes:

Communication with parents

(*1*) When and how would you communicate with parents?   1....2....3....4....5
(2) Describe how you would conduct a parent conference.   1....2....3....4....5
(3) Would you be willing to have parent volunteers in your classroom?
     (If so, what might parents do?)   1....2....3....4....5
(4) Can you share an example of a positive communication with a
     parent that enabled you to help a student?   1....2....3....4....5

Notes:

Cultural awareness of today's students

(*1*) Describe today's students (at the age you will teach).   1....2....3....4....5
(2) What problems and stressors might these students have?   1....2....3....4....5
(3) How do you motivate students to excel academically?   1....2....3....4....5
(4) Where do you turn to find help for your students and their
     problems?   1....2....3....4....5
(5) How will you promote acceptance, tolerance, and cultural
     diversity in your classroom?   1....2....3....4....5
(6) A hypothetical question for this category. (e.g., What would you
     do if a student were sleeping in your class?)   1....2....3....4....5

Notes:

Professional questions

(*1*) Why have you chosen to apply in this district?   1....2....3....4....5
(2) How do keep current with your specialty (reading, math, etc.) and
     with the field of teaching?   1....2....3....4....5
(3) How do you feel about being assigned a mentor teacher during
     your first year of teaching here?   1....2....3....4....5
(4) How do you combat stress?   1....2....3....4....5
(5) What was the most important part of your teacher education
     program?   1....2....3....4....5
(6) What is your greatest strength as a teacher?   1....2....3....4....5

Notes:

Wrap-up and other questions

(*1*) What do you expect from your colleagues and supervisor?   1....2....3....4....5
(2) What questions do you have for us?   1....2....3....4....5
(3) Overall interpersonal communication skills (ability to present
     themselves to the interviewer).   1....2....3....4....5

Notes:

Total   39 questions × 5 = 195

Figure 2 (continued). Interview checklist/evaluation.

BEGINNING THE INTERVIEW

Always be professional and courteous, greeting the candidate with a handshake and a smile, offering them a comfortable seat. If your secretary/support staff member has not already directed them to available restrooms, you should do so. With regard to offering coffee or a soft drink, let common sense be your guide. Some employers begin with a tour of the facilities, using the tour to explain the size of the school, class size, the specific assignment that is open, and highlights of the school. As the employer you are not only looking for the best candidates, but you are recruiting them to work for you. The very best candidates will have several options open to them and you need to sell your school to them. Recent graduates want to feel "recruited," even if they have just driven only two miles from their campus dorm for the interview.

If you don't begin with the tour, you may want to begin the interview by telling the candidate about your school and the position opening. Be sure to tell the candidate the format of this interview—whether it is the only interview, a preliminary interview, or one of two required by the district. Inform the candidate about how you will ask questions, take notes, or record the session. If it is obvious that the candidate has brought a portfolio, let them know that you encourage them to share specific examples from their portfolio as you ask questions, and that you would like to allow some time to review the portfolio at the end of the interview as well.

One or two general icebreaker questions will do just that—break the ice and build rapport between the candidate and the interviewer. The first few questions should set the stage, reduce the initial tension of the interview, and put the candidate at ease. Opening questions may include:

(*1*) Tell me about yourself.
(*2*) I've read your resumé. What would you like to tell me now that we are meeting, that is not on your resumé?
(*3*) Your resumé indicates that you completed (something special, such as varsity baseball, junior year abroad, overseas student teaching, chess tournament champion). Before we begin with the nuts-and-bolts questions of the interview, would you tell me a little about your involvement with _____?
(*4*) What made you choose teaching as your profession?

Be prepared for the candidate to comment about your office and about a trophy, plaque, or desk ornament, since that is an easy way to make small talk. (Again, these questions are in checklist/evaluation format in Figure 2.)

QUESTIONS FOR KNOWLEDGE OF TEACHING/SUBJECTS

What makes a good teacher? Ask a dozen teachers, teacher educators, and administrators and you will get a dozen different answers. However, teachers need a knowledge of their chosen subject matter and a knowledge of teaching in order to be effective. Much of your interview should focus on questioning the candidates about their knowledge of pedagogy and of the subject matter. You will evaluate the candidates' answers, either formally with a quantitative scale or informally with a general approach. For some of your questions you may be looking for a specific answer, but for other questions you will be looking for an answer that shows you that the candidate has background in a given area and has studied the area. Some candidates may share teaching ideas that are new to you, and those ideas may be rated very highly by you. Let's look at some sample questions and what some strong and weak answers to those questions would include. These and other questions are listed in the interview checklist/evaluation at the end of the chapter (Figure 2).

What Should the Curriculum Be for This Grade/Subject Area?

A strong answer for this question would show evidence that the candidate has worked with the grade level, is familiar with trends for that grade, and can discuss skill acquisition as well as the role of textbooks in the curriculum. Giving specific examples from past experience provides strength to the answer, such as "At my last school we spent two months writing curriculum outlines. I learned that curriculum includes strategies and philosophies as well as specifics of when children are capable of learning a certain topic." The candidate can elaborate, explaining how what we teach and how we teach are very important to the learning process.

Average answer: "When I student taught at this level, we used the ABC reading series and the XYZ math series. If I am hired here, I would start to build my curriculum around those two series, since I have had experience with them."

Weak answer: The candidate may ask, "When you ask about curriculum, do you mean which textbook series am I familiar with?"

How Will You Design Unit Plans for Your Teaching?

Strong answer: "I like to do both long-term and short-term planning and unit plans are my long-term plans. Unit plans make the most sense when they relate to what the students know and are interested in, and also when they go across the curriculum. For example, a unit plan about the Revolutionary War can relate history and literature so easily. Unit plans are like my flight plan from 20,000 feet above sky level. I'll write my lesson plans from ground level!"

Average answer: "It's always good to group things. Teaching Spanish it's easy to have unit plans. You teach a unit about food, then one about animals, then one about towns. You can build a new unit around whatever the vocabulary is."

Weak answer: "This is my second year of teaching and I learned last year that you can plan all the units you want, but you have to just really work on keeping the students busy and getting through the textbook. Maybe this year I'll have time to actually plan units."

The questions about lesson planning, models of teaching, and teaching strategies are very important. Strong candidates will not only be able to name models of planning, but will show you a sample plan from their portfolio. They will talk about the importance of getting the students' attention with a novel introduction or anticipatory set, the value of modeling and showing examples, and the importance of getting students to actively do things with the new material. A strong lesson plan has a review, and the teacher builds some type of assessment into the plan to see if the students learned what was taught that day. Another strong answer would be one where the teacher tells you about a specific plan that he/she wrote and implemented, detailing how the students reacted that day and how much they learned. An average answer includes a reference to learning to write plans in college, maybe in the Madeline Hunter style, and then an explanation that the teacher now writes what needs to be covered and writes about any special materials in the plan book. The average answer may end with, "Any substitute could read my plans and would know where we were with the material." Be very concerned if the candidate tries to convince you that the best teachers really don't write lesson plans—this is a weak answer!

Strong candidates will be able to talk about models of teaching for their particular field and will be able to talk about which strategies motivate students to learn. For example, a reading teacher must be aware of the whole language-phonics debate. A foreign language teacher should be able to talk about the pros and cons of the total immersion approach. Math teachers should be able to discuss the standards published by the National Council on the Teaching of Mathematics, and the topic of teaching with story problems.

How Do You Begin a Class? What Are Some Good Techniques for Ending Class?

Strong answer: "I like to begin and end classes in a variety of ways. I always have an assignment or brain teaser on the board for students to get started on immediately. I make sure that they are working before I take a quick attendance check with my seating chart. I put an outline of my lesson plan on the board, too, so they know what we will cover. After a while they learn that my review questions at the end of class are often my test questions, and that helps keep them focused all the way to the end of the hour. I also like to end by asking students to write the famous "one-minute papers" about what they learned. It lets me know in a non-graded way if they did get something out of that class."

Average answer: "I make sure everyone is there and that they have their pencils and books. It takes time but I believe in getting them settled. I try to follow my plans, getting as much done as I can and keeping them busy. I try to review or help them start their homework, but sometimes the bell catches us at the end."

Since you are employers, I probably do not have to share examples of weak answers—you have probably already heard them all!.

Continue your interview by asking about homework, grading, and meeting the individual needs of students. Strong candidates will be able to defend their answers, and that is important. A candidate who can explain the need for homework to you can explain it to parents. A teacher who can give examples of ways to help slow learners while also challenging the gifted students in the classroom has insights needed to survive in the classroom. When you ask, "What are some characteristics of effective teachers?," some candidates may talk about a favorite teacher from their past. This may be a strong answer or a weak answer, depending on what the candidate says. If the candidate says, "Miss Mathis was the most effective teacher I ever had because she got everyone to like her," it is definitely a weak answer. If they describe how Miss Mathis encouraged them as individuals, covered the material and made it interesting at the same time, attended regional conferences, developed their creativity, and got everyone to respect her, then that is a strong answer.

CLASSROOM MANAGEMENT

Successful classroom management and discipline remain at the top of the list of challenges for beginning teachers (Gordan, 1991; Veenman, 1984). Beginning teachers must have a starting point for their classroom management, or the students may literally take over early in the year. A teacher with a plan is proactive. He/she observes an outburst in the classroom and is prepared to deal with the behavior. A teacher without a plan will react to each and every incident. Students will test the reactive teacher to see how far they can go before pushing him/her over the edge (Canter and Canter, 1993).

With Which Classroom Management Writers or Theorists Are You Familiar?

A candidate should be able to discuss the work of at least two writers. Since Lee Canter is so famous, most should be able to discuss his work. In discussing the work of those who write about classroom management, a strong answer will include pros and cons of each.

How Would You Create and Implement a Classroom Management Plan?

The principal of a large elementary school told me that he asked this question of all finalists in interviews. He expected to hear strong answers such as, "I would create my plan from the best of Lee Canter's work, the best of Harry Wong's work, and what I have read about 'Discipline with Dignity.' I would have posted rules and every parent would have a copy of our rules, consequences, and positives. The first week of class would be spent getting the students to understand that we are a classroom and that the rules are 'our' rules. I would try some group meetings to create the rules, guiding the students to what would work for all of us. I would teach a lot of routines. I would encourage students and always use their names. I would try to 'catch them being good' and reinforce good behavior immediately."

One candidate reached for her portfolio, opened it to the page of rules, positives, and consequences, and gave this answer, "During student teaching, I worked with my cooperating teacher as we developed these rules in her classroom. In fact, I made the poster that was the large version of this sheet. My coop teacher sent this letter to everyone, and it's a good model for one I will send to parents. I saw these rules developed and implemented. We changed one rule that wasn't working, but the rest worked well all semester. In your school, I would tailor these rules to your districtwide policies about detentions and sending students to the office, but you get the idea of where I would begin. I really do believe in getting off to a good start. I believe that getting to know the students and their interests will help a lot with management and that clear communication of expectations is important." She was not only hired, but the contract to her was extended at the end of the interview.

Candidates should be able to discuss which rewards and consequences are appropriate for the age of the student. While eating lunch with the teacher is generally considered a big-deal reward for a first-grader, it is definitely a punishment for a sixteen-year-old! Ask how the candidate will communicate the classroom management plan to students and parents, as well as ask for specific examples of past experiences with management, since few candidates may share the near-perfect example described earlier.

A weak response will indicate that the teacher is not anticipating any problems and is simply going to go in and "be the students' friend." "If a problem arises, I'll think of something at the time. I'm not a fan of too much structure." I have seen these new teachers in many of my seminars. They are frantic by the end of October and ready to quit teaching by May, if indeed they have survived that long. They rarely get a chance to teach what they intended to teach because all of their time is spent "putting out fires" around the room. They blame the students and the parents, and are very frustrated and unhappy. All teachers will have to find a balance between complete laissez-faire in the classroom and unreasonably strict discipline. A teacher who begins with complete laissez-faire may not survive long enough in the classroom to find an appropriate balance.

Hypothetical Situations for Classroom Management Questions

(*1*) What would you do if one of your students threw his/her books down on the desk and yelled, "I hate this school. I hate this class and I hate you, teacher?"
(*2*) What would you do if a student called you a very foul name?
(*3*) What would you do if a student threw his/her desk against the wall of your classroom?
(*4*) What would you do if two students continually chattered during your class?
(*5*) What would you do if a student tripped another student?

COMMUNICATION WITH PARENTS

Communication with parents is not only closely related to classroom management and discipline, but the two are interrelated. If a candidate has not addressed communication with parents when talking about classroom management, then ask the question directly, "When and how would you communicate with parents?" Ask the candidate to describe how they would conduct a parent conference. Ask about their experience and willingness to have parent volunteers in the classroom. Ask them to share an example of a positive communication with a parent that enabled them to help a student.

QUESTIONS REGARDING CULTURAL AWARENESS OF TODAY'S STUDENTS

Student teachers and first-year teachers with whom I have worked often comment that today's students are "streetwise," "wise beyond their years," "easily distracted," and "starved for positive attention." Teachers admit that students are often noisy, rude, impatient, and unwilling to do work that "isn't for a grade." Yet, successful teachers know that they must be respectful of all students, regardless of their backgrounds, and treat all students with care (Haberman, 1995).

When you ask a candidate to describe today's students, do not be surprised by some negative responses. In fact, strong teachers will be able to discuss the problems and stressors that the students present in their lives. When asked what problems second-graders might have, a teacher should be able to discuss the affects a divorce or poverty have on children. A new high school teacher should know how drug and alcohol abuse can affect classroom behavior and performance. In asking about cultural awareness of students, you are looking for teachers who are aware of the myriad problems facing today's youth, and yet believe that they can make a difference in these students' lives. Strong answers contain references to the teacher's persistence in working with noisy, rude students and to the teacher's understanding that today's students do not necessarily walk into classes "ready to learn." For example, a candidate who explains that many children come to school without breakfast, and who further explains that she worked with her former principal and kitchen staff to develop a small food pantry to provide children with dry cereal in paper cups, understands the problems and is going to work to solve them.

Even as teachers comment on today's "wild and crazy" kids, they must absolutely comment on the strength and hope that today's students bring into schools. One high school teacher commented, "I know that most of my juniors and seniors work. I'm impressed when a student who works thirty hours a week can still maintain a B average. Think about how much that student could do if he gets a college degree and a good job. I would want to hire him. My job as a teacher is to encourage him to further his education, and to make sure he has the skills to do so." That is such a strong answer, compared to "It's really hard to teach students who are busy working in fast-food restaurants thirty hours a week." A really strong answer would be, "Because so many of my students will work outside of class, I'm going to use their job experiences whenever I can. They can figure an annual salary based on their actual salary and then we can figure budgets in my math classes. We can discuss what kinds of homes they can buy on those salaries. I'll bring in statistics on what a college graduate would make, versus what high school graduates will make over a lifetime. Those numbers are so staggering that they make anyone want to stay in school."

All candidates can tell you "war stories" of the tough situations children may face today. Strong candidates will go beyond the problems and tell how education will make a difference for these students, and that the teacher can be a role model and motivator for all students. Again, look for specific examples. Ask candidates *how* to motivate students to excel academically. Ask teachers where they might turn to find help for their students. Ask how the teacher plans to promote acceptance, tolerance, and cultural diversity in the classroom. Hypothetical questions for this part of the interview could include:

(*1*) What would you do if a student were sleeping in your class?

(*2*) How will you react if a student calls another student a racially offen-
sive name?

(*3*) How will you react if a student calls you a racist?

PROFESSIONAL QUESTIONS

Last year, my husband changed jobs. So, after being an educator in
Illinois for eighteen years, I found myself sending resumés to colleges
in the metro-Atlanta area. Even though I had indicated in my cover letter
why I was moving to Georgia, every interview I had included multiple
versions of the question, "Why have you chosen to apply *here?*" I made
use of the question to stress what I had learned about the college, as
well as reiterating that my spouse and I were relocating permanently to
the area. I occasionally made a small joke about not wanting to shovel
snow in the winter anymore. This seemed to be what employers wanted
to hear and I was hired. The truth is that I gave the answer to one of
the discriminatory questions that can't be asked (marital status) in my
answer, but I volunteered the information. The fact is that I needed a job
in that geographic location and I did not want employers to think I was
"fleeing" my home state for any negative reasons.

Why do candidates apply in your district? Probably because you have
a job and they want a job! Some candidates are relocating because of a
spouse's transfer or job change. Many candidates are applying because
of your district's reputation. For others, it may be the chance to get their
first job. Again, the answer isn't as important as the candidate's ability
to answer.

The answers to other professional questions are perhaps more important. Asking candidates how they keep current in their field of teaching
will give them yet another chance to demonstrate their enthusiasm for
their subject. They should be attending at least one conference a year
and reading at least one professional journal. Because of finances, some
new graduates will report that they are not currently active in their professional organization, but plan to reactivate when employed.

If your district has a mentor program, inform the candidate about
your program and invite them to participate. It would be a "red flag" if
a candidate said, "I don't need a mentor. I've been teaching two years
since student teaching and I know how to do it." This candidate probably
would not be a team player, nor would he/she be interested in new ideas

or team teaching. It is hoped that a strong candidate would be interested in any opportunity to learn and grow—including having a mentor teacher with whom to share ideas, joys, and successes.

Since teaching is considered a high-stress job, it is good to ask the candidate how he/she combats stress. A strong answer might include a reference to walking after school, exercising, doing aerobics, or getting together with friends. If the candidate laughs and gives a clever answer such as "Sometimes we just have to laugh, go home and hug the dog, then start fresh the next day," I would also give that a high rating, since a sense of humor is good stress relief. This is an ambiguous question. How would *you* answer it in an interview?

Asking "What was the most important part of your teacher education program?" should bring some interesting responses. Most new teachers cite their student teaching as the most important part of their college program, because they were out in the field and doing so much "real work." As a teacher educator, I know that many students rate their classroom work as "too philosophical" or "too impractical." I think that the important part of the answer to this question is how the candidate supports the answer. A strong answer here would have a strong "because." For example, "Student teaching was the most important part of my program *because* in student teaching I was able to try out the theories I studied in college. It was neat to know that my cooperating teacher would observe me, give me feedback, and not let me get too lost. It was good to be able to talk about a plan with the coop before I implemented it. Student teaching was like team teaching, and it never hurts to have two people sharing ideas and strategies." Someone who is totally negative about their college preparation may be negative about other aspects of their life and work.

THE STRENGTH/WEAKNESS QUESTION

Interviewers generally ask the question, "What is your greatest strength as a teacher?" I like this question and feel that the response gives the candidates another chance to sell themselves. Many interviewers ask the opposite of this question, "What is your greatest weakness as a teacher?" I feel that everyone has weaknesses, but that in an interview we all need to focus on positives, so I would not include this question. As with any interview question, if you can find a reason to ask the question, and then have some standard by which to evaluate it, that question will be valuable to you.

WRAP-UP QUESTIONS

Eventually, you do need to close an interview. In order to begin the close, you might ask, "What do you expect from your colleagues and supervisors?" Strong candidates will tell about positive interactions with colleagues in the past, perhaps a team-teaching experience or one where they co-planned an activity such as parents' night. Very strong candidates will state that they hope that evaluations from their supervisors help them to grow as teachers. They can talk about preconferences, observations, and postconferences as part of the clinical supervision cycle (Glickman, 1985). Someone who talks about the advantage of having an administrator in the room to serve as "another pair of eyes" is giving a strong answer, since they recognize that the administrator is focusing on student performance.

This is also a good time to explain the specifics of salary and benefits. Be honest and specific. Do not apologize for salaries or make comparisons to other districts. If your secretary or support staff member is also the recordkeeper for insurance and benefits, let that person join the interview to explain the district's package to the candidate.

QUESTIONS FROM THE CANDIDATE

You always need to allow time for candidates to ask questions. If you have not already covered points such as class size, assignment of duties, and salary base, candidates will ask about them. Candidates will probably also ask about sports teams, standardized test scores, and any special events for which your school is noted. They may ask about your time frame in hiring, what other materials you need from them, and when they will find out your decision. If you tell a candidate that you will call on a certain day, then you must do so. Allow plenty of time to get back to a candidate. If you do not know when you will be able to get back to them, tell them so, but realize that they may take another job in the interim.

There will come a point when both parties realize that the interview is over. Shake hands, direct the candidate back to the front door, or parking lot, and thank the candidate for the time spent interviewing. Even if you do not plan to hire this person, be cordial and friendly. When the candidate has left, finish your evaluation and notes before you forget the details of the interview.

OTHER INTERVIEW INSTRUMENTS

As stated, the questions in this chapter are designed to help interviewers develop their own checklist of questions and an interview evaluation. Some commercially developed interview packages exist, and your district may want to review some of them. As with any materials marketed to schools, you will need to evaluate the cost versus the value for your school. Some questions to consider when looking at commercially prepared interview packages include

(*1*) How was this program developed? Were the developers practicing teachers, administrators, and/or educators?
(*2*) What is the per-person interview cost? Can forms be copied?
(*3*) Is anyone else using this program? Is it so common that university instructors will be teaching the questions to their students?
(*4*) Is the interview package easy to administer and easy to adapt for teachers of preschool through high school?

POST-INTERVIEW SCENARIOS

"I was told by an interviewer that she would get back to me on Monday. When she had not called by Wednesday, I called and was told that the process was taking longer than expected, and it would be another week before they could contact me with a specific answer. I had another offer and accepted it. Did I really want a boss who said one deadline and did not use it? I, of course, informed the school that I had accepted another offer. The school called two weeks later and asked if I had signed a contract. The interviewer said she still wanted to hire me, if I was available. I stuck by my decision to stay at the school where I had already accepted a verbal offer, even though it was a loss of $3,000 in salary." Is this case typical or extraordinary? This type of discussion seems to go on endlessly at some schools. Some beginning teachers will accept your offer verbally and keep looking for a better one. How quickly can your district send a formal letter of intent or a contract to a new hire? How badly do you want to hire someone who agrees verbally and then declines your offer for another?

Ann, a recent graduate in math education, has accepted your offer to teach junior high math and has signed a contract. She continues to look for positions in insurance and ten days before the first day of school, she calls your office to inform you that she has accepted a position with a large company. She regrets the inconvenience to your school, but she cannot turn down the salary offered by the business. What is your reaction on the phone? Will you pursue the matter with your district's legal service? How will you fill the position?

You have just completed an interview with Sam, a candidate who has done fairly well with your questions. Before leaving he asks, "What did you write about me on your notepad? I really want to know, especially if you've written something that may prevent me from being hired." What is your reaction to Sam?

QUESTIONS FOR DISCUSSION

(*1*) The candidate begins the interview as a very aggressive used-car salesperson might—selling himself/herself and not even giving you a chance to ask your questions. What is your reaction to this candidate?

(*2*) The candidate appears VERY nervous, so nervous in fact that he/she can hardly sit still. Should you continue the interview? Should you ask if there is a problem? Should you act as if nothing is wrong? What is your reaction?

(*3*) You have just asked a candidate what his/her greatest weakness is as a teacher. The response is "It bothers me when students are late. I wouldn't belittle them or anything, but I would give them a dirty look as they enter the classroom with their passes." How do you evaluate this answer?

(*4*) When asked why she choose to apply for a fifth-grade position at your school, Sandra replies, "My advisor said that there would be 75 to 150 applicants for every elementary position opening this fall. She said I should apply for every opening, even ones in small schools like yours." She pauses, smiles, and has no further answer. How do you rate this answer?

(*5*) During an interview, Jamie begins to cry. She says that she is sorry for her emotions, but that it has been a rough semester and she is very anxious about getting her first job. She excuses herself for about ten minutes, washes her face, and then returns to the interview. What is your reaction to this scene? (Author's note: The personnel director of a large school district told me that this really happened and that the candidate was actually hired! The director said that the teacher remained in the district for two years, filling a tough special education position. While she wasn't evaluated as an extraordinary teacher, all of her evaluations were above satisfactory and no negative comments were ever reported about her.)

KEY POINTS

(*1*) Develop a set of questions that can be used consistently in interviews.

(*2*) Interview questions should assess the candidate's knowledge of teaching skills, of the specific subjects to be taught, of classroom management, and of parent communication.

(*3*) Questions to assess the candidate's awareness of the diversity of students and of professional issues should be included.

(*4*) Questions need to be asked in a manner that can be evaluated by the interviewer.

(*5*) The interviewer needs to develop a checklist and/or other system to record the pertinent information from the interview in a usable format.

CHAPTER 6

Group Interviews

THERE ARE ADVANTAGES and disadvantages of using groups to interview and hire teachers. We have all heard the old saying, "Two heads are better than one." This means that two people brainstorming together can think of more possible solutions than one person sitting alone and trying to solve a problem (or deciding which candidate to hire). However, we have all also heard the saying, "A camel is a horse built by a committee."

COMMITTEE WORK

Many people like to work in groups and committees. They find the give and take of dialogue and open discussion to be invigorating and conducive to decision-making. They like to think aloud and listen to others do the same. They want to hear someone else's opinion of a candidate's answer and of a candidate's background. It can be argued that group interviews are more open and democratic. How can teachers complain about a new hire when they were on the selection committee? If a new hire turns out to be ineffective, it may be easier to say, "Everyone on the committee voted to hire him/her," than to say, "He/she was hired because he/she interviewed so well with me."

Other people do not like any type of committee work. They find it to be time-consuming and ineffective. Many teachers feel that they are asked to work endless hours on a committee only to have the administration do whatever they wanted to do anyway. Taking teachers out of their classrooms to interview prospective hires costs money in terms of substitutes, and taking time away from teachers' planning time is difficult, too. Administrators often feel that they could hire new teachers much more efficiently without waiting for the committee to schedule meetings and debate the candidates' qualifications. They worry that confidentiality issues will not be maintained if several others see all the materials of the candidates. Just as former president Harry Truman had a sign on his desk that said, "The buck stops here," so too must somebody be the designated person to make a decision about new hires.

Many districts are so large that all hiring is done by personnel directors who are professionals in hiring and management. Yet, personnel directors and principals cannot be expected to know everything about every grade level and every subject. As my first principal did, they may want to get some input from a teacher specializing in the area, such as foreign language.

EXAMPLES FROM DISTRICTS

Some districts do indeed use committees successfully. They have a policy that as many as five to six teachers from each school be that school's hiring committee. The committee meets throughout the year to determine hiring needs, envision new positions, write the job descriptions, and sort the applications that arrive. They do the interviewing and make a group recommendation to the board about the new hires. The principal may chair the committee and conduct a one-on-one interview with each candidate separate from the group's interview. (I know of at least one district where the principal is a committee member but does not serve as chair.) A teacher who serves on one of these committees told me, "It's like rush was at my sorority in college. It's a tremendous amount of work, but we know that we are part of the decision-making process and because our input is used, it's worth it." One of the building secretaries attends all committee meetings and takes notes. The secretary does all of the follow-up letter writing to applicants. For consistency, the chair calls the candidates to make the offers.

To make this type of hiring process work, the policies have to be crystal clear to everyone involved. The board and central administration have to be supportive of the system. The teachers on the committee must make a large time commitment, some of which will take them out of their classes. Everyone involved needs a thorough understanding of the illegal-questions issues, affirmative action, and of the need for confidentiality. Arrangements must be made to pay these teachers for summer work, since much hiring will probably take place over the summer. Coordinating schedules may be the toughest part of using teacher committees for hiring. Why would a teacher *want* to serve on such a demanding committee? It's probably the best possible step for a teacher to gain experience to became a full-time administrator or personnel director. A teacher may want to serve on the committee to fulfill an internship requirement for an advanced degree, or may simply feel that it is important work to do as a professional. The building principal must be willing to accept that the decision of the committee may be different from his/her individual decision might have been. Again, there are advantages and disadvantages. If the committee conducts the actual interviews, then the candidate needs to be aware of this when first invited to interview, as stated in previous chapters.

INTERVIEW QUESTIONS FROM THE GROUP

The committee should have a master list of questions, and each member should ask the same questions of each candidate. Committee members need training and orientation about how to respond to candidates in the interview situation. For example, they need to know about restraining their responses, both verbally and with their body language. If a candidate announces in an interview that she never plans to give a letter grade to students' work, this may shock a committee member who believes that every piece of paper needs a grade. The committee member has to realize that he/she should not look or sound indignant about this situation. The interviewing committee members will certainly have differences of opinion with some practices voiced by candidates, but the group interview is NOT the time to voice that philosophical disagreement or to debate grading procedures. Committee members have to keep their disagreement internal, noting the candidate's response for later discussion among the committee. When committees discuss candidates' responses, they must have a chairperson who can keep them focused. I've been a teacher and I've served on enough committees to know how easy it is to get off track and begin to debate side issues. The committee must focus on objectively evaluating candidates' responses, not on debating the pros and cons of every issue brought up in the interviewing questions. In my own mind I can envision committees that NEVER get around to making a hiring recommendation because of continual, endless debate of related side issues. I've also served on committees that made excellent hiring recommendations in a reasonable amount of time. It all depends upon who serves on the committee and how well the group is led and focused.

If you use a committee, who should serve on it? How will your district choose the teachers who will participate in this process? Just as when hiring a new teacher, remember to begin by following the district policies and union agreements already in place. You want to advertise the responsibilities of the committee, request that those interested complete an application, and then evaluate those who apply. One job of the interviewing committee may be to name their replacements each year. Having only half of the members leave at the end of any given year will help to provide continuity. A two-year term for members, with half of them leaving at the end of each year, may be a good way to keep consistency and to avoid burn-out of members at the same time. Above all, the first committee meetings should be dedicated to orientation to the hiring processes. The teachers, even if they are department chairs and/or trained in administration, need training that is specific to how to hire. (Give them all a copy of this book and create a library of resources for them about interviewing.)

There can be variations on the theme of hiring by committee. The central office's personnel department may hire all new teachers, then have them interview with a committee of teachers at the different schools in the district to determine placement. Again, you can probably see all kinds of challenges with this, but the advantage is that each school feels that they have had input into their new faculty. The biggest challenge is the confidentiality factor involved with committee recommendations. Consider that a committee at Lincoln School has interviewed four newly hired teachers and they unanimously request Sally B. for their first-grade opening. Sally B. is assigned to Carter Elementary and Lincoln School gets Renee for their first grade. Several committee members bemoan the fact that they did not get Sally B., and even Renee hears that she was not their first choice. What does this do to collegial support of the new teacher at Lincoln School? In other words, how would *you* feel if you were Renee?

USING MORE THAN ONE INTERVIEWER, BUT NOT A COMMITTEE

While interviewing by committee is probably the most democratic method, it may also be the most time-consuming. If you are interested in getting other opinions during the hiring process, but do not want to use the full committee method, there are other options.

In one district with which I worked the assistant superintendent coordinated all hiring for the district. All applications were received and reviewed first by him. He conducted screening interviews by telephone.

He conducted personal interviews in his office. When principals were available, they were invited to join him for the interviews. Since all interviews were videotaped, he could review them at a later date and make specific ratings of candidates. He routinely sent the videotapes to the principals, both for their input on whether or not to hire and for their input about the placement of newly hired teachers (there were many elementary schools in the district). For example, he sometimes had to hire a dozen or more new elementary teachers. He would begin the sorting processes, hiring some and getting feedback from the principals with regard to the placement of them. As positions filled, he might send four tapes to a principal and indicate that the principal could select the one new teacher still needed for a vacancy from the group. That one teacher would then be offered a contract. One advantage of this system was that the assistant superintendent had time—whole days when necessary—to devote to the hiring process. Unlike the building principals, he was not running the day-to-day events of a large school while squeezing in time to screen and interview candidates. Principals were invited to attend recruitment fairs with the assistant superintendent as well. The assistant superintendent's office had support staff who could devote time to organizing files, handling inquiry calls from candidates, and helping the newly hired teachers complete all their paperwork (insurance forms, tax forms, etc.). The assistant superintendent also coordinated the new teachers' orientation, induction, and mentoring (more about this in Chapters 10, 11, and 12).

CENTRAL OFFICE COORDINATION OF INTERVIEWING

When one person in a central office coordinates the hiring, the principals can still have much positive input. The central office and principals need to have clear, scheduled means of communicating. Monthly meetings are good, with bi-weekly or weekly meetings during peak hiring times. If application files can be evaluated by the building principals, that can provide much help to the central office. Again, the central office does the first sort, eliminating incomplete files, noncertified people, and so on, so that the principals are evaluating the best of the applicants, and the ones with the most experience for the current openings. If a personnel director and three principals evaluate applications with the same rating instrument, then the top few candidates should surface. It is good to try this and begin to see the similarities and differences in evaluations by different employers. The central office can coordinate hiring, with the building principals conducting the final interview and making a recommendation to the central office. The principals can be spared some of the time-consuming details of the hiring process, while still having input and feeling that they are finding the best possible candidates.

With high school hirings and some specific elementary positions, the process may take an even more complicated twist, as those positions require specific subject matter knowledge. If the central office and principals are communicating and evaluating applications, it can be very beneficial to add the department chair and/or a veteran teacher to the process. The central office can narrow the search to five applicants, the principal can narrow to three and the department chair can interview and evaluate those three. Foreign language is a specific example where a subject matter specialist may need to be consulted. In foreign language, someone should interview the applicant in the language to be taught. Even a ten-minute interview will yield a fair idea of how well the applicant actually speaks the language. No one person can be a specialist in everything. If I were hiring science teachers, I could evaluate their knowledge of general pedagogy, but not of the specifics of their field. I would definitely want another science teacher to conduct a short interview with them to determine if they really knew their chemistry and physics.

The subject matter specialists and veteran teachers can help in other ways too. Reading specialists who attend professional conferences will meet other teachers who are completing advanced programs such as Reading Recovery and can recommend those teachers to you. Veteran teachers who serve as cooperating teachers to student teachers can give you an in-depth evaluation of a newly certificated student teacher. However, a word of caution must be given here. Your district does not want to rely upon only "insider information" for hiring. You will want to formalize how you request information from your specialists. One way to do this is to send out listings of openings to all teachers in the district and to include a form that those teachers can use to make a recommendation. Hopefully, this will prevent a teacher from saying, "Mrs. Davis hired Mike Smith only because Mrs. Kline said he was so wonderful. My student teacher was much better at teaching social science than Mike Smith, but I didn't get a chance to bend Mrs. Davis' ear about him. I guess I'm not in the inside circle."

When should the hiring process be completed by individuals and when should the process include others or be done by committees? There is no one simple answer. It is important to remember that the school board actually hires the new teacher, and that the committee chair, the principal, and the superintendent make the recommendations. The factors involved include the number of new teachers to be hired, the amount of time allocated for someone to be a hiring agent, the availability of a pool of teachers in your area, and the climate that exists between the central office administration, the building administration teams, and the teachers themselves. All involved must be aware of the importance of hiring the best qualified person for the job and of the necessity to hire based upon fair and equitable standards.

SCENARIOS FOR ROLE-PLAY

These scenarios can be used for discussion, but also for training of committee members new to the hiring process. To use the scenarios as role-plays, assign roles to participants and have them say the lines that they would use in a conversation with the persons listed. It can prove very helpful to practice what one would say in a difficult position!

(*1*) As a middle school principal, you have relied upon Mrs. Torres to be a dependable substitute teacher. She is in the building often and there is never a problem when she substitutes. You have encouraged her to apply for a full-time sixth-grade position that has opened. She is interviewed by you and by the lead teacher for the sixth-grade team. Your interview goes as expected and she remains your top choice for the position. When you and Ms. Hopkins (the lead teacher) discuss your evaluations of the three interviewees, you are surprised that Ms. Hopkins ranks Mrs. Torres as her third choice. She is adamant that Mrs. Torres is not academic enough. Yes, she is friendly and dependable, but look at her college grades compared to those of the other candidates. Also, when Mrs. Torres subbed for Ms. Hopkins, some students said she gave them three answers to a test and said that the test was hard for *her*. How will you react to Ms. Hopkins? Of the three candidates, who will get your recommendation to the superintendent for hiring? Traditionally, you and Ms. Hopkins are the ones who conduct interviews and have input on the new sixth-grade hires. (Play the roles of Ms. Hopkins and the principal. If they cannot come to an agreement, to whom should they turn next?)

Next, the superintendent joined the hiring process and recommended that Mrs. Torres not be hired. The candidate that Ms. Hopkins rated as the top one is recommended for hiring and accepts a contract. Mrs. Torres requests a meeting with you after receiving notification that she was not selected for the position. What will you say to her? Have someone play an angry Mrs. Torres and make you, the principal, defend the district's position. How much of your opinion will you share? How much of the hiring process will you share? *Remember to be careful here. We live in the litigious 90s. Choose your words carefully.* Would you send Mrs. Torres to the superintendent? Do you think that she will go there next anyway? How has your professional relationship with the lead teacher been affected by this?

(2) There are five teachers and one principal on the building-level hiring committee. There were 123 applicants for a second-grade position. The central office and the committee of principals narrowed the applicants to four, all of whom had student taught in the district, substituted in the district, or had a strong letter of recommendation from a well-known teacher in the district. After spending hours interviewing all four applicants, the committee is tied between Carol and Gina. Carol is a mother of two, divorced, and a dynamite substitute. It could be said that she lobbied hard for the interview and for the second-grade position. She has three years of full-time experience from a nearby town where she taught before starting her family and she has glowing letters of recommendation. Gina also has three years of experience in a neighboring school district. She student taught in your district and she and her cooperating teacher remain friends, even attending conferences together. Her recommendations are also great. You know that Gina has always wanted to return to your school for a job. Your district pays somewhat more than where she works and she would not have to drive so far to work. She is single. You and two teachers support Gina. Three others support Carol for the position. There may not be another opening for several years at second grade at your school. Role-play three people defending their choice and three people defending the other choice. How can you recommend one teacher? How can you keep the debate from becoming unprofessional and too personal?

(3) You have spent days interviewing three candidates for a high school position to teach German. Miss Walton is your first choice. She is from a neighboring state, has had a lot of experience teaching in culturally diverse settings, and even won an award during student teaching. She lived one semester in Graz, Austria. However, the chair of your foreign languages department, a native of Germany, says that Miss Walton does not have a good command of the language. She

recommends that you hire Mr. Schild, a man who grew up speaking German in his home. Mr. Schild's grades are not nearly as good as Miss Walton's. His teaching style seemed very laissez-faire in the interview and he could not articulate how he would plan for classes well at all. Should you hire Miss Walton or Mr. Schild? The decision is entirely yours, as you have asked the foreign language chair for input, but do not necessarily have to use what she says. Role-play what you would say to the department chair if you still choose Miss Walton. (You may be a principal or a personnel director.)

How much does subject matter count and how much does knowledge of teaching count? Foreign language will not be the only "special case" where this issue surfaces.

(*4*) Mr. Kyle is a new teacher but decided to teach after taking a very early retirement package from General Motors, where he built cars. He is certified and has applied to be the new shop and automotive teacher. He knows cars like the back of his hand. He has raised two sons and has a daughter in your school. His interview does not go well because he does not know the buzz words in education. He can't talk about inclusion, behavioral objectives, Madeline Hunter, and so on. He admits in the interview that he did not get much theory out of the education classes, but that he knows he can "win kids over." He said that student teaching was difficult because he did not understand why kids didn't want to work—especially on cars. He says that every student who talks back should learn some discipline and be kicked out of class until they do.

The only other candidate is Mr. Jason, a twenty-three-year-old graduate with average grades. He says that he ended up in the technical education program because he took a lot of shop classes in high school and he really liked his teachers. He's quiet and soft-spoken and says he will work hard. His student teaching evaluations are mixed, with the cooperating teacher writing that Mr. Jason knew more about writing lesson plans and the history of education than most professors, but less about cars than the students.

Who will you recommend for hiring? Why?

DISCUSSION QUESTIONS

(*1*) If you were hired in a newly created school district that had no history of "this is how we hire teachers," what kind of policies would you develop for the hiring of new teachers?

(*2*) How much control should the principals and administration have in hiring? How much control should the teachers and their unions have? Is the process ever completely fair and equitable?

(*3*) If you have just been hired as the personnel director of a school district, how could you begin to implement some of your idealistic policies?

(*4*) In many colleges and universities, students get the opportunity to interview candidates for professorships, deanships, and even presidencies. Should your students get to meet the candidates who are being interviewed for new positions? Is is possible due to schedules? Would it be a worthwhile experience for the candidates and the students?

KEY POINTS

(*1*) If a committee is used in the hiring process, make each member's role clear from the beginning.

(*2*) Committee members need training in how to interview candidates and in the issues of discriminatory questions.

(*3*) Make use of the strengths of those already working in your district. Central office administrators can help streamline the process of interviewing. Principals must be involved. Department chairs and lead teachers can be valuable assets.

(*4*) Some people are simply not committee people—don't force anyone to serve on a committee who doesn't want to!

CHAPTER 7

Portfolios, Videos, and Other Supporting Materials

AN ARTIST TRYING to get a show in a gallery meets with the owner and shows examples of past work. Aspiring actresses and models have stacks of best photographs to take with them to interviews. An architect brings a collection of drawings to share with a potential client. All of these examples and collections are portfolios, and educators have learned the value of sharing portfolios in order to further showcase their experience and expertise. Candidates who bring a portfolio to the interview and use it successfully to explain their credentials will probably also have students create portfolios of their own work. Candidates with portfolios recognize that showing someone may be a better way of explaining (teaching) than just telling someone.

As an employer, you may request a modified portfolio with the application of a prospective teacher. If you do so, outline exactly what you want to see and let candidates know that the modified portfolio should consist of copies, not originals. If you plan to keep the portfolio, let the candidates know. Again, you want a minimum of paperwork, so this may not be the option for your district to take. However, if you do want to see a sample lesson plan, a sample management plan, and additional letters of recommendation that outline specific duties (coaching, etc.) you may want to request a portfolio. When requesting this type of portfolio attached to an application, limit it to specific topics of your choosing and never more than six to ten pages in a paper folder.

The most typical teacher portfolio is one that the candidate brings with him/her to the interview. This portfolio is a three-ring binder and provides evidence that the candidate has some experience and has taken the time to organize and present examples of experience.

What is in a typical portfolio?

(*1*) A current resumé
(2) Copies of all transcripts

(3) Copy of teacher certification or application for teacher certification (If you have not received official copies of these, the candidate can take them out of the binder and your office can make a quick photocopy.)

(4) Additional letters of recommendation that highlight specific duties, such as coaching, activities sponsor, or community involvement

(5) Sample lesson plan from student teaching or first-year experience

(6) Sample letters to parents that have been sent in the past

(7) Outline of classroom management plan

(8) A sample unit plan that outlines how the teacher taught one major unit in the grade/subject level

(9) A few pictures of bulletin boards, student learning centers or special events while teaching

(10) Copies of some student work

(11) Copies of certificates of appreciation or awards

(12) Proof of memberships in professional organizations or attendance at conferences

Some students may also include their personal philosophy of education statement, or the mission statement from the school where they student taught.

The portfolio should help you see how a given teacher organizes things. The portfolio should also help the candidates present themselves. The candidate should not use the portfolio as a crutch, turning to it every time you ask a question, but rather use it occasionally to reinforce what is being discussed. All candidates, both those teaching elementary and secondary students, should be able to explain how they might use portfolio assessment in the classroom with their own students. Parents want to see students' work and teachers need to be able to help students showcase that work.

While presentation is important, don't let a beautiful portfolio wow you into hiring a teacher who may be weaker in other areas. Just as the resume and cover letter present the candidate, so does the portfolio. Some people may be better suited to writing and creating great "scrapbooks" than they are at standing in front of energetic youth and starting a class. Some teachers may have great interpersonal skills and be able to work tirelessly with students, but cannot create the picture-perfect portfolio. Some colleges of education simply may not be giving their students orientation about how to build a portfolio. At this point in time, the portfolio remains a very nice "extra" for the candidate, and may help you as you interview many individuals.

VIDEOS

Chapter 5 outlined your use of videotaping the interview with the candidate. Some candidates may want to send you a video of a previous teaching experience to further showcase their abilities. It is common for student teachers to be videotaped during their student teaching semester. Often such videotaped lessons are used for evaluation by the college supervisor. Candidates who are moving from another state due to the relocation of a spouse may want to include a videotape as an "extra."

The first questions to be asked when you receive a video is, "Am I going to evaluate this?" and "If so, how will the video be evaluated?" The candidate should include a written memo about the video, including when it was made, for what purpose, and who the students were in the classroom. They should list the length of the video and include a short lesson plan so that you get an idea of what is going on before you start to review the tape.

For what elements should you be watching? Just as if you were in a classroom, you will want to look for interpersonal communication skills—eye contact of teacher to students, voice loud enough to be heard by students, and general positive skills in front of the class. You will also want to evaluate if you can follow the flow of the lesson. Is there an introduction? Does the teacher explain why the material is important and how it relates to the lives of the students? Do the procedures of the classroom seem to move along in a timely manner? Are the students actively involved? Is there variety? Does the teacher make some kind of conclusion to the lesson and/or assess what the students learned? Does the teacher appear overly anxious or nervous?

A video is one way to see the teacher "in action" without ever leaving your office or bringing the candidate in to your district. I have evaluated many videotapes made by pre-student teachers and student teachers and I find that the video is a good tool because I can rewind and review. I use videos to evaluate teachers' questioning skills and to look at higher-order questioning. Videos are also great tools to help teachers to see themselves as their class perceives them, and if a teacher has a problem with saying "um" or "ok," a quick look at themselves on camera may solve that problem.

As with everything, a word of warning is appropriate with regard to the evaluation of videotapes. Plan to do some sort of mental evaluation of the tape to decide if the person is really teaching or just acting for the camera. While teachers need some of the same skills as actors, we do not want someone who is only acting and cannot really manage a classroom. Many people look great on camera and others of us just do not, yet we may still be good teachers! Also, you have been working in education long enough to decide if the students are being themselves or acting from a script.

WHAT THE FUTURE HOLDS

Many faculty and staff of colleges and universities are now sending the supporting materials for jobs via the internet. Engineers and those in high-tech fields are doing the same. Cover letters, resumés and letters of recommendation can be e-mailed to their destinations. Time is saved and the receiver can sort online and decide which credentials to print and which candidates to interview. With more and more computers being connected with mini-video cameras, people can conference over the internet with relative ease. Videoteleconferencing will much easier than dealing with videotapes from individuals. As the technology spreads, more and more people will have access to it and have the knowledge to use it. A person's web page will tell you a lot of information about him/her. Your web page can be used to share a lot of information about the available position.

QUESTIONS FOR DISCUSSION

(*1*) In your search for a computer technologist for your school, how much will you weight how the candidates send their supporting materials (i.e., via the internet or via mail)? Should this "weighting" factor be included in the original job description and advertisement?

(*2*) If anyone in your class has videos of themselves teaching, bring those in and evaluate them as an employer might. After the critiques are in, would you send your video to a potential employer?

(*3*) You have interviewed four candidates and all seem exceptionally well qualified for a position. Only one brought a portfolio and it was a model one. Would this affect your final decision?

(*4*) You have interviewed four candidates and all seem exceptionally well qualified for a position. Only one brought a video and it showcased a well-taught class. Will this video be the deciding factor for you?

(*5*) We cannot and should not discriminate in hiring because of physical characteristics. Would requiring a video to be sent with supporting materials give employers a chance to discriminate against individuals because of race or physical characteristics such as weight problems before the chance to interview?

KEY POINTS

(*1*) A candidate with a portfolio recognizes that documentation is important and uses the portfolio as a visual aid to further explain teaching strengths.

(2) A video from a candidate may give you a clear example of some teaching skills.

(3) As technology continues to advance, we may use electronic letters, videoconferencing, and other innovations in the hiring process.

CHAPTER 8

Final Decisions and Final Negotiations

ADD UP THE POINTS (QUANTITATIVE EVALUATION)

After all of the supporting materials have been evaluated and all candidates have been interviewed, how will you decide who to hire? One option is to keep every evaluation an objective one and to hire the candidate with the highest number of total points. Another option is to rank the candidates in several areas—their points from the supporting materials, the interview, and your overall "feeling." Sometimes one teacher will stand out as being the most experienced overall, but not have as much specific experience with one criterion of your job description. Should this be a weighted factor in your decision? When the committee is deciding to make a recommendation, there should be a clear policy. For example, the candidates' points will be tallied for half of their ranking and then each committee member will create a ranking of their own. The members' rankings will be weighted and then the top candidate will be nominated for hire.

Example

Candidates can score 50 points from their pre-interview evaluation of paperwork and 195 points from their interview checklist, totaling 245 points. Each of five committee interviewers will rank the candidates 1 through 4, with each 1 receiving 20 points, each 2 receiving 15, each 3 receiving 10 points and each 4 receiving 5.

Candidate A earns 240 points from materials and interviews, and is ranked first by three committee members ($20 \times 3 = 60$ points), second by one (15 points), and third by one (10 points). The total score is 325.

Candidate B earns 230 points from materials and interviews, and is ranked first by two committee members ($20 \times 2 = 40$ points), second by one (15 points), and third by two ($10 \times 2 = 20$ points). The total score is 305.

Candidate C earns 200 points from materials and interviews, and is ranked such that he/she earns 50 points, totaling 250.

Candidate D earns 190 points plus 40, totaling 230.

It is obvious that candidate A has been rated at the very top by this system, although two committee members did not rate him/her as their first choice. It is also obvious that a candidate with the highest scores from two evaluation instruments and chosen as the top candidate by three of five committee members would be the one top candidate. This system gives some "quantification" to the process. Most committees would probably have come to the same conclusion, but allowing a written ranking from the members and then adding the numbers probably saves hours of committee debating. The point to consider here is whether or not the job would be extended to B if A has already accepted a job elsewhere, and if the job would be offered to C and D if the higher rankings have also accepted positions.

HOW DO YOU FEEL ABOUT THE CANDIDATE? (QUALITATIVE EVALUATION)

If you alone are making the final recommendation of whom to hire, you may still feel like Tevia in "Fiddler on the Roof" as he debated with himself, saying, "on the one hand ... yet, on the other hand ..." Your qualitative evaluations should help, as should your own experience. A friend of mine related a story of hiring a new counselor. Candidate A was overqualified, possessing not only certification, but a Ph.D. She said in her interview that she wanted to leave her hectic city practice and saw the school position in a small town as much less busy for her. She was very "thorough and clinical." The other finalist was not as overqualified on paper, but possessed the correct certification and fantastic interpersonal skills. This candidate made the interviewer feel happy just talking with her. My friend hired the second candidate and said, "If I or one of my children were in need of a counselor, this is the person to whom I would turn." She said she never once regretted the decision. Can you use the question, "Would I want this person teaching my own children?" in your decision-making process? Many interviewers do.

Question to Consider

Two candidates seem equally well qualified. One appears to be single and a twenty-two-year-old recent graduate. She has shared in her interview how much she appreciated her parents and their help as she obtained her college degree. The second has shared that she is a single mother with a three-year-old baby and has put herself through the last two years of college after dropping out when she became a mom. To whom would you extend the job offer? Should you be considering the sympathy factor? Will candidates tell you personal information to get a sympathy vote?

The purpose of this book has been to stress the importance of evaluating a candidate's ability to do the job *of teaching*. This includes evaluating lesson plans, organizational skills, teaching experience, and interpersonal skills. Some interviewers still "get to the heart" by looking at the whole person and his/her personal background. The decision of how personal to be is left up to each employer, and some believe that they will always hire by "that little inner feeling."

Hopefully, all of your hiring decisions will be between two or more well-qualified candidates. If, after all of the materials and interviews are evaluated, no one candidate appears best, then you must decide if you will hire the best of those who did apply or begin a new search. Many administrators tell me that this happens about one day before classes are scheduled to begin!

ONCE THE DECISION IS MADE

Once the decision is made, let the first-choice candidate know your decision and give them a timeline for accepting your decision. This is the time to recruit verbally and make the candidate feel appreciated and sought after by your school. Unlike in universities and corporations, a lot of salary and related negotiations generally do not take place at this time. The candidate should already understand the salary and teaching assignment. Some candidates may begin limited negotiations about assignment of classes or about which particular classroom will be theirs. Imagine the ill will created by stories of "the new teacher" demanding and getting "the biggest classroom" or of a veteran teacher being asked to relocate to a smaller, colder classroom and you see a clear picture of the problems of these types of negotiations! Remember to define the position early and to articulate the position and expectations throughout the interview to avoid such misunderstandings at this stage of the hiring process.

Be prepared for some of the top candidates to say no, especially if you are in an area experiencing a lot of growth in schools. Be prepared to offer the position to the next candidate, yet do not let him/her know that they were not the first choice. Again, verbal recruitment will not only make the candidate feel special, but will begin a positive relationship with that employee. Gossip generally runs wild in schools during peak hiring periods; limiting the information given to the rest of the faculty will save hours of headaches later on. When candidates accept verbally, follow up with written confirmation as soon as possible. If you must wait on school boards to meet to make an official contract, you may want to consider sending a letter of intent to the new hire for a signature. A letter of intent can also include an outline of benefits offered to the candidate. Benefits are a big concern for new employees and failure to explain benefits may cause problems. Let the candidates know before the job offer is made if the benefit package is dependent upon passing a physical. If the candidate accepts the position and must then pass drug testing or a police background check, be sure that those stipulations have been explained both verbally and in writing.

Once the candidate accepts, put their name on a mailing list for all of your updates about the new school year. When the candidate has signed the contract, your job is half over. The next half of building the best faculty is the induction process.

DISCUSSION QUESTIONS

(*1*) Share scenarios that you are aware of regarding the final negotiation phase of hiring. Have any candidates said or done something after the contract was offered that made the employer question the hiring decision?

(*2*) What will you do if the candidate tries to "play hardball," accepting your offer, but then insisting upon a different assignment or classroom? For example, the new science teacher says that he/she signed the contract understanding that three of the sections he/she would teach would be honors classes rather than general earth science.

(*3*) Your office contacts the first-choice candidate on Monday and that candidate says that he/she needs a week to consider the decision. One week later, the same candidate still insists on needing more time. Do you make another deadline or withdraw the offer? How long will you wait?

(*4*) How can you minimize rumors about the hiring process from circulating?

KEY POINTS

(*1*) Evaluate candidates based upon their ability to do the job of teaching.

(*2*) Once a hiring decision is made, begin "verbal recruitment" to initiate a positive work relationship with the new teacher, and complete follow-up paperwork immediately.

(*3*) Place the newly hired teachers on your mailing list for summer updates.

(*4*) Work to mimimize the gossip that surrounds the hiring of a new employee.

CHAPTER 9

Problems of Beginning Teachers and the Need for Induction

DO YOU REMEMBER your first year of teaching? I certainly do. I taught more of my minor area than of my major. The room was too hot, too small, and too dirty. Why did I have to have such a bad room when the veteran foreign language teacher had such a nice room? I arrived early, stayed late, and took lots of work home. I felt unprepared for the "type" of students who were coming into my so-called college-bound classes. How could I teach Spanish grammar to students with no grasp of English grammar? I was totally unprepared for how to respond to students selling drugs, or for dealing with those students who were assigned to my study hall instead of jail. I always asked myself, "Why don't the students come into my class excited to learn?" I soon began to ask "Why don't they have a pencil?" "Am I the babysitter?" "How could my evaluation say that I'm too academic? After all, I'm teaching an academic subject!" I worried constantly about the "right" and "best" ways to present material, to test students, to average grades, and to motivate the unmotivated. I felt that I was the first high school foreign language teacher to grapple with these questions. What were my policies for classroom management and discipline? I thought I was super calm and super patient—winning my students over was my plan and I didn't begin to think of posting rules and being so formal. (This, by the way, did not work very well.) Fortunately, as the first few years progressed, I found some mentors, both in the school and from outside the school, to help me reflect upon my teaching, the job itself, and most importantly, the students. When I began to attend Saturday workshops, take some summer classes, and talk about my teaching, things miraculously improved.

The boundless enthusiasm and the "change-the-world" attitude of beginning teachers should not be overlooked. While I began this chapter with all of my first-year complaints, the first year was a pivotal year for me, and one that helped to shape my teaching career. There were more positives than negatives. I truly believed that everyone in my classes could learn enough Spanish to travel and live abroad, if they so chose, and I encouraged them to do so. I was excited about going to work every day, and followed up on every single student's absence. After all, I *wanted* them to be there and to learn. In my work with beginning teachers, I have seen over and over again the same boundless enthusiasm that I felt. It usually includes a burning desire to learn and to improve as well. One new teacher in my class wrote, "There is so much that I learned this year and so much more that I want to learn. I can hardly wait for the summer to end so I can begin teaching again!" As an administrator, you not only want to hire this person, but also to *keep* this person on your faculty. Hopefully, her enthusiasm will infect others on your staff.

When I began graduate school, I realized that my initial years of teaching were very typical. I also began to realize that school districts must work to keep teachers in the classroom, through ongoing staff development programs and improved conditions in the school as a workplace. When more and more teachers leave after only a few years of teaching, the district faces increased time commitments to hiring new teachers. In addition, complaints from the community about staff turnover rates will hurt both morale and school reputation. The teaching profession cannot afford to lose approximately 50% of newly hired teachers during the first five years of their careers, which is estimated to be the case (Gordon, 1991; Huling-Austin, Odell, Ishler, Kay, and Edelfelt, 1989; Haberman, 1995).

WHY ARE TEACHERS LEAVING THE PROFESSION?

Many new teachers say that the first year of teaching is often a trial by fire, and that they are left alone to "sink or swim." A beginning teacher in one of my programs said she felt as if she had been hired and then "thrown to the wolves." Another said the experience was more like being "thrown into the lions' den." In addition to figuring out how to survive at their new positions, teachers are very stressed about earning a living, paying their bills, and succeeding at the job for which they went to college so long. Many are also trying to teach in a way so as to combat social injustice, to go "against the grain" of just being a comfortable teacher who teaches the safe and routine way (Ayers, 1993, p. 3).

PROBLEMS OF BEGINNING TEACHERS

The problems of beginning teachers are real and do exist (Dollase, 1992; Gordan, 1991; Veenman, 1984). The recurring problems include classroom management and discipline, motivating students, dealing with students' problems, insufficient supplies and materials, dealing with special needs students, insufficient time to prepare, and working with parents, administrators, and community.

In 1996 I surveyed 150 beginning teachers who were completing their first or second years in the classroom to assess their problems, stress, and intention to remain in the teaching profession. These teachers were all graduates of one regional midwestern university and included preschool through high school teachers. One-third of the teachers were elementary teachers, 22% were teachers of junior high/middle school, 27% were high school teachers, 9% were unitwide teachers (band, art, traveling special education, or similar), and 9% did not indicate their grade level. The highest rated problems from this group included motivating students, dealing with students' social and emotional needs, classroom management and discipline, and dealing with the large numbers of students in classes. Table 1 represents results of this survey.

The teachers in this survey rated their perceived stress levels on a scale of 1 to 7, with 7 representing the highest stress levels. Overall, the teachers rated their stress during the first year of teaching at 5.20 and the second year at 4.07. Table 2 represents the data for each set of teachers completing the survey.

A 1993 article about combating stress cited the most stressful job in America as "inner-city high school teacher" (Butterfield, 1993). A teacher with high stress may not be as effective as one who feels the task of succeeding is attainable. A teacher with high stress may not be able to distinguish minor problems from major ones—all problems may begin to look insurmountable. Stressed teachers may have lower self-esteem and be afraid of everything that the supervisor and parents say to them. They need to feel somewhat comfortable and confident in order to become more confident in front of the classroom.

Table 3 presented here from my 1996 research includes the responses of the 150 first- and second-year teachers to the statements regarding enjoyment of teaching, confidence, and intention to remain in the teaching profession. This group of teachers seemed to really enjoy teaching, felt fairly confident about their teaching, and indicated that they did not intend to leave the profession at a drop-out rate of 50%.

Table 1 Means of Ratings of Problems Encountered.

	pK–6	Jr High	High School	Unit	Other	All
n	(50)	(33)	(40)	(13)	(14)	(150)
(1) I have had problems motivating students						
150	2.78	3.30	4.08	3.23	4.07	3.40
(2) Dealing with students' social and emotional problems is very difficult.						
150	3.74	3.21	3.35	2.54	3.29	3.37
(3) I have had problems with classroom management and discipline.						
150	3.19	3.06	3.31	3.27	3.57	3.24
(4) The large number of students in my classes presents a problem.						
147	2.98	3.41	3.30	3.17	3.71	3.24
(5) Having enough books and materials is a problem for me.						
150	2.96	3.45	3.13	4.15	3.07	3.23
(6) My classroom is uncomfortable -size, temperature, cleanliness.						
150	2.58	3.21	2.80	3.23	3.29	2.90
(7) Working with special education or inclusion students has created problems.						
143	2.75	2.86	2.46	2.00	4.07	2.76
(8) Grading students' work has been a problem.						
147	2.49	3.00	2.72	2.00	3.43	2.71
(9) I have had problems communicating with parents.						
150	2.52	2.42	2.48	2.77	3.00	2.55
(10) I have had problems dealing with the administration of my school/district.						
150	2.18	2.73	1.98	2.88	2.57	2.43
(11) I have had problems with presenting and teaching the subject material.						
148	2.31	2.39	2.44	2.15	3.00	2.41
(12) I have had problems working with other teachers.						
150	2.10	2.24	1.83	2.54	2.43	2.13

Note: On this survey, a 1 indicates strongly disagree and a 7 indicates strongly agree; therefore, the higher the number, the greater the problem was rated. All items are listed here as they appeared on the original survey instrument.

QUESTIONS FOR DISCUSSION

(1) Administer the survey from Table 1 (or one you create yourself) to your faculty. How do the answers that they provide compare with those listed here? Are there any differences between beginning teachers and the veteran faculty?

(2) How would you have rated the problems listed when you were a first-year teacher?

Table 2 Means of Ratings of Teachers' Stress During First Two Years.

	pK–6	Jr High	High School	Unit	Other	All
n	(50)	(33)	(40)	(13)	(14)	(150)
My first year of teaching was/has been stressful.						
149	5.22	5.52	5.03	4.96	5.14	5.20
My second year of teaching was/has been stressful.						
87	3.97	4.29	4.32	3.44	4.00	4.07

Note: On this survey, a 1 indicates strongly disagree and a 7 indicates strongly agree; therefore, the higher the number, the more stress the teacher felt. All items are listed here as they appeared on the original survey instrument.

(3) On the scale of 1 to 7 used in Table 2, how would you rate the stress you felt the first year of teaching? What else was going on in your life when you were a new teacher?

(4) How many of your newly hired teachers will be relocating to your town from another city? Another state? How can your district ease the relocation process and the stress of moving? How many are newly-weds and/or new parents?

Faced with a myriad problems, as well as high stress, the question becomes "How can we keep beginning teachers in the profession?" My answer is in the form of an essay I wrote in 1997, after a very interesting seminar.

Table 3 Means of Ratings of Teachers' Perceptions of Enjoyment of Teaching, Confidence, and Retention in Profession.

	pK–6	Jr High	High School	Unit	Other	All
n	(50)	(33)	(40)	(13)	(14)	(150)
I really enjoy teaching.						
150	6.28	6.27	5.40	5.62	5.07	5.87
I feel confident about my abilities to be a good teacher.						
150	6.16	6.17	5.92	5.31	5.79	5.90
I see myself remaining in teaching until retirement.						
149	5.73	4.86	4.68	5.35	4.57	5.11
I see myself leaving teaching during my first five years.						
150	2.02	2.06	2.51	2.81	3.21	2.34

Note: On this survey, a 1 indicates strongly disagree and a 7 indicates strongly agree. All items are listed here as they appeared on the original survey instrument.

How Can We Keep Beginning Teachers in the Profession?

As the coordinator of the Beginning Teacher Program at my university, I teach over fifty seminars annually to first- and second-year teachers in school districts. The curriculum for my seminars includes how to become established in the classroom, approaches to classroom management, communication with parents, teaching strategies, motivating students, and stress management. I always allow time during my programs for the new teachers to express their joys and concerns, anything from major problems to personal successes. I have found that this type of sharing can be vitally important to the teachers, helping them to combat isolation in the classroom and often giving them a venue for creative problem solving.

Recently, a veteran teacher attended one of my all-day sessions for first-year teachers. She wanted to refresh some of her own skills and her principal had encouraged her to take a professional day, learn what she could, and then perhaps serve as a mentor for first-year teachers. The veteran smiled as the ever-so-young rookies introduced themselves by telling the group what a typical day was like in the classroom. She listened attentively while the new teachers talked of the difficulties of large numbers of students in their classes and of multiple preparations, such as the first-year social studies teacher with six fifty-minute classes to teach every day, and each class was a different subject. As the teachers participated in an activity titled, "How do *you* learn best?," the veteran witnessed teachers who really did believe that all children can learn. These bright, hard-working newcomers not only believed in teaching with a variety of strategies to meet the needs of the students' diverse learning styles, but were well equipped with good ideas for doing so. (At this point the veteran was busy writing down some nuts-and-bolts ideas that the new teachers were glad to share.)

As the day progressed, the veteran witnessed even more first-year war stories. She heard the new teachers' stories of cleaning their own classrooms, buying their own supplies, and battling stifling hot classrooms and then bitter cold classrooms. They spoke of having to deal with irate parents, sick students, mounds of paperwork, and the fear of not being rehired the second year. One teacher said that her first evaluation was very low because she had students working in activity groups when she was evaluated. Her principal said that the next time he visited, the students had better be in rows and that she had better be "really teaching." Many expressed concern about not knowing how to deal with the social and emotional problems that the students were bringing with them into the classroom. Dealing with the special education and inclusion students came up often in the group discussions, as did the worry of retaining students and finding ways to motivate the unmotivated.

Yet, even as the problems seemed insurmountable, this group of new teachers appeared even more determined to face the challenges and "change the world" of education. One high school physics teacher related his story of working as a janitor at a large company after school and discovering old computers in the trash. He retrieved them and put them to use in his classroom. A third-grade teacher said that after only seven months of teaching, she now knew that she would become a principal some day so that she would be able to empower her teachers to do the best possible teaching for their students. A middle school teacher said, "There is so much that I have learned this year. I just can't wait to start all over again next fall and do an even better job." As the beginners left, the veteran stayed behind to ask me, "How can we keep these bright, talented, energetic, and dedicated young teachers in the profession?"

We can begin by paying them fair salaries that will allow them not to have to hold second jobs in order to teach. We can give them smaller numbers of students in their classes so that they can personalize instruction and implement some of the many textbook solutions that they know. If they are teaching middle and high school sections, we can give them fewer numbers of preparations, so that they can prepare creative activities that engage students. We can make sure that classrooms are cleaned and well cooled and/or appropriately heated. We can give teachers the books, supplies, and supplemental materials that they need, as well as updated computer technology. More psychologists, social workers, nurses, and counselors should be working in the schools, so that children can be ready to learn when they get to the teacher.

Once the basic necessities are taken care of, we can then turn to the staff development side of this question. We can train principals in clinical supervision methods that will make supervision a tool to enhance and improve teaching behaviors. We can create environments where the new teachers do not plan their lessons in isolation, but do so with a team of other teachers. Schools should have professional libraries and staff development monies so that continual learning is a part of teaching. We shouldn't ask teachers to work all day and then sit in inservice programs after 3:30 P.M. Let's embed staff development and make it ongoing and continual. All new teachers should have release time to attend seminars and support groups. Let's also make sure that all new teachers have trained mentors who can help answer their questions. After all, everyone needs a sounding board to help them reflect upon what's going on in the classroom.

Colleges of education and education professors need to recognize that their roles do not end when the student completes student teaching and receives a diploma. Learning to teach is a continuum, and it might be said that the entire first year of teaching is truly a "teachable moment" for the new teacher. Every college of education needs at least one person who is out working with the graduates—researching their problems and providing a network of support. Colleges need to continue to strengthen their ties to the schools and practicing teachers, so that on-campus classes and real-world experiences are even more closely connected.

"Is any of this actually possible?," queried the veteran. Of course, it's possible. Not only is it possible, but it is imperative if we are to have a qualified, professional teaching force. If we can create an environment in schools that helps first-year teachers to survive, that same environment will also help veteran teachers to succeed. As teachers, administrators, colleges, and communities strive to reform education, let's remember to reform the environment in which all teachers work. A positive school environment paired with vital staff development will keep beginning teachers in the profession.

While staff development will help teachers to learn new strategies for teaching, gain new ideas for classroom management, and help them cope with stress, staff development does not help a teacher to overcome poor conditions of the workplace. When beginning to plan an induction program for your newly hired teachers, always ask, "What are the needs of these teachers?" And, even more importantly, "Can these needs be met with staff development?"

WHAT IS INDUCTION?

Induction is the planned staff development for new teachers, and for those who are new to a school or district. Beginning teachers need induction into the school, the district, and the profession. Teachers who are new to a school or district will still need induction into that particular system. One definition of induction follows:

> Induction is an effort to assist new teachers in performing—that is, expressing their competence in the particular context to which they have been assigned—toward the end of being effective. Through induction, new teachers continue to form and refine their images of themselves as teachers in terms of their competence, performance, and effectiveness. (Mager, 1992, p. 20)

In addition to defining what induction is, Mager stipulates what induction is not:

> Induction is not a process in which the deficits of the preparation program are to be remedied. Nor is induction a means of teaching the neophyte everything that needs to be known for a lifetime of practice in the "real world." Induction is not simply the experience of socialization of the new teacher to the local culture of teaching. And induction should not be the extension of a screening process. (1992, p. 20)

Regie Routman makes six recommendations for supporting new teachers:

(*1*) Where mentor teachers are available, free them up for modeling and meeting new teachers' needs.
(*2*) Create opportunities for collaborative planning (between novice and experienced teachers).
(*3*) Provide release time to observe quality teachers.
(*4*) Provide professional reading relevant to the district's curriculum.
(*5*) Role-play curriculum nights and parent conferences.
(*6*) When possible, apprentice new teachers before they begin teaching. (1996, p. 138)

The goals of teacher induction are:

(*1*) to improve teaching performance
(*2*) to increase the retention of promising beginning teachers during the induction years
(*3*) to promote the personal and professional well-being of beginning teachers
(*4*) to satisfy mandated requirements related to induction and certification. (Huling-Austin, 1989a, p. 16)

DOES SUPPORT FOR BEGINNING TEACHERS WORK?

Can the goals of teacher induction be met? Will creating a support program actually improve a teacher's effectiveness and help to retain that teacher in the profession? I recently had the opportunity to hear Dr. Harry Wong speak. Dr. Wong makes the most convincing case for teacher induction that I have ever heard, by sharing true stories in his workshops. In his book he writes, "Without help and enculturation, beginning teachers perpetuate the status quo by teaching as they remember being taught. And if we do not reach these teachers, they will in turn listen to the same people with the same message and have things validated in the same way, and we will repeat the same cycle generation after generation in education, going nowhere" (1998, p. v).

Individual research reports are very positive about the results of induction programs. Wilkinson (1994) summarizes such research, "Researchers found that these induction programs supported the beginning teachers during the stressful transition into teaching to reduce the numbers leaving the profession. Colbert and Wolff (1992) found that 95% of the beginning teachers who experienced support during their initial years remained in teaching three years. Odell and Ferraro (1992) reported 80% of the supported first-year teachers remained after five years" (p. 53).

Schelske and Romano (1994) found that "Highly stressed teachers tend to behave differently from teachers who report low levels of stress. Highly stressed teachers are more hostile and less supportive of students . . ." (p. 21). Support seminars for new teachers can provide stress management techniques, enabling teachers to be more supportive of their own students, which enhances effectiveness.

To summarize, induction can be thought of as an umbrella covering three areas—orientation before the school year begins, support seminars for the new teachers that are held throughout the first (and possibly second) year, and the mentoring of new teachers by trained veteran teachers. The next three chapters cover each of these areas.

DISCUSSION QUESTIONS

(*1*) How can you assess the needs of newly hired teachers to plan for their induction? Can you survey the teachers who have just finished their initial years to gain information?

(2) If the problem is too many students, not enough books, or not enough space, how can your system remedy those problems for new (or veteran) teachers?

KEY POINTS

(*1*) Capitalize on the boundless enthusiasm shown by beginning teachers.
(*2*) Recognize that beginning teachers will have problems, but that planned induction and support will help them to cope with the challenges of the job.
(*3*) An effective teacher induction program will help teachers to improve their performance while promoting personal well-being.

CHAPTER 10

Orientation

EVERY SCHOOL HAS back-to-school orientation for teachers. It varies widely from district to district and from state to state, but generally lasts from one day to one week and includes all-district and all-building faculty meetings as well as a time set aside for the teachers to work in their classrooms. Some orientations are social and festive, with the local chamber of commerce hosting a back-to-school appreciation breakfast for all faculty. Some districts make back-to-school meetings the time to charge up the faculty and bring in motivational speakers. Others limit whole-group meeting times and concentrate on specific curricular meetings, planning for grade- and subject-level meetings and work times. Whatever the content and delivery of the orientation, it is vitally important to promote time for teachers to network with each other and for them to work in their classrooms. All newly hired teachers will need to be involved in the faculty orientation, so the first rule for new teacher orientation is *not* to schedule it during the regular back-to-school orientation programs.

INVITE TEACHERS TO ORIENTATION

Invite the new teachers to attend their orientation activities as soon as they are hired. In fact, tell them of your district's orientation during the interview process. Be specific about the dates of orientation, whether it is mandatory or not, and whether or not they will be paid for attending those days. (If it's not mandatory, some new hires will not attend.) In many districts the orientation days and payment for them are bargained by the teachers' union, so plan the time and budget for this orientation into the next contract. Again, the earlier new teachers are hired, the more settled they will feel as they begin the orientation. They more settled they feel, the more they will be able to gain from the meetings.

If orientation is so crucially important, why do some teachers go out of their way to find an excuse not to attend? Why do others bring their knitting or sit in the room reading a book? Why do some teachers bring a pencil and start writing the names in their grade book and penciling in dates and plans in their plan book? Why do the coaches sit together and draw team plays? What are their excuses? "If it's on a handout and in our handbook, why does the principal spend this much time reading it to us also?" "I don't need another so-called expert to tell me to be excited about working with kids. All I need is more time to work in my room and to get things started my way."

For new teachers, the lines are a little different. "I'm not a new teacher by any stretch of the imagination. I'm just new to this district." "This is boring. In college they told us to be wary of the teachers' lounge and of any group meetings. They said we would have to just figure out the real rules from the veterans and our close friends." "I can't sit in a meeting NOW. I've got to get the water turned on in my apartment so I can take a shower." "How can I learn all this new stuff instantly? Nobody told me I had to fill out sixty-two forms to work here." "I just picked up my class rosters and I don't understand how I can have thirty-four students in this class. When I interviewed, they said the average here was twenty-six."

THE GUIDELINES FOR SUCCESSFUL NEW TEACHER ORIENTATION

The guidelines for successful new teacher orientation will also make all faculty meetings go more smoothly.

(*1*) Make sure that all participants get the same information regarding date, time, and place. There will always be people who show up early and late, but if you follow the published plan, things will run more smoothly. Orientation is NOT something that takes place at the end of a hectic first day of school. It must occur during the school hours, when the students are not present. Start on time!

(2) Make the environment comfortable. I once delivered the keynote address for a districtwide back-to-school orientation in a cafeteria that was about 100 degrees Fahrenheit. The teachers had to sit on very uncomfortable cafeteria benches. Coffee was served as the

beverage. Would YOU like to listen and learn in that environment? Nobody would.

(3) Introductions are important and necessary, but remember that new teachers will remember only the people that they absolutely need to know. They need to know the district personnel for benefits, the secretaries, the janitors, and the faculty who will help them to deal with special ed, counseling, and other special services.

(4) Icebreakers and get-acquainted games are only as good as you make them. One of my favorite activities for new teacher orientation is to have each new teacher introduce himself/herself the way they plan to introduce themselves to their first class on the first day of school. They are to tell us who we are (first-graders or sophomore English, etc.) and then role-play to us as they would their class. Some beginning teachers have never thought of what they will say the first two minutes of class, so this activity gets them thinking!

(5) Refreshments are a must, but please give a choice. As someone who does not drink industrial-strength coffee, I always appreciate fruit juice or mineral water as a choice. I've noticed that many teachers under age thirty start their day with diet soft drinks, even as early as 7:30 A.M. As much as I would like to eat a sugary doughnut or cream-filled pastry, my diet won't permit it, and I'm thankful when a low-fat bagel or a banana is offered.

(6) Everyone loves freebies. Give your faculty a nice pen or a set of magic markers or something to welcome them back. Try to give the new teachers a welcome bag with as many items as possible. Items may include post-it notes, a calendar, markers, and other items needed for teaching. One district included some humorous items—a sample of aspirin, a free ticket for a cafeteria lunch, and three quarters for a soda from the machine.

(7) Limit time in seats. After twenty minutes of welcomes and introductions, have teachers stand up and do some aerobic exercises (and remind them that their students need to do this, too). Give breaks. If you don't, teachers will leave anyway.

(8) You have a lot of material to share or you wouldn't need an orientation! When you need to teach a lot of information in a short amount of time, use active learning strategies. Present the material in a variety of ways. Be creative. Announce that you will speak for six minutes and that an egg timer will go off at the end of that time and that the teachers will then have one minute to talk with the

person seated next to them about what you just said. Divide the meeting into four groups. Have each group read one-fourth of the material on a certain handout and be ready to present their material to the group. Don't read handouts to teachers! Have them read sections silently and discuss those sections with two other people in a group. You see the idea here. Hopefully the teachers will use these strategies as they present new material in their classrooms. Move around the room. Use your best teaching strategies in the meeting and teachers will listen. How many times have we told teachers that today's students do not enter the classroom, sit down, and start learning? Teachers have to motivate students and we have to motivate teachers. Modeling good presentations and good teaching will help to do that.

(9) All orientations need to be evaluated by the participants. Neither veterans nor new teachers will be silent about their needs. Conduct written evaluations and use the feedback for better programs in the future. A program *planned* by teachers and administration and *presented* by teachers and administration will better meet the needs of all teachers.

(10) Lastly, always ask yourself, "What did I want to know when I was I new teacher?" Teach those things and have other teachers present those items. Some beginning teachers have reported that they feel intimidated and overwhelmed by twenty-year veterans providing their orientation and have suggested that second- and third-year veterans provide survival tips, ideas, and suggestions.

In his book, *So Where's My Apple? Diary of a First-Year Teacher,* Glenn Walter recommends that new-teacher orientation sessions be delivered one week before the regular faculty meetings. The structure should include morning group sessions followed by afternoons spent in the classroom. New teachers can meet the school board at a breakfast or luncheon.

Many models exist for orientation. A good rule to remember would be, "inform, but don't overwhelm." It is always a good idea to go from the general to the specific, meaning that orientation programs begin with districtwide meetings, then building-level ones, and eventually the meetings become subject- and grade-level specific. Give the teachers a notebook with all the new material, so they can use that as their reference all year long. A list of ideas for the new teacher notebook will be given later. Let's look at a sample multi-day orientation for new teachers.

NEW TEACHER WORKSHOP—ANYTOWN
SCHOOL DISTRICT

Day 1—Morning session for all new teachers
Where: Board room of the administration building
Presented by the personnel director and/or assistant superin-
tendent

(*1*) Breakfast for all new teachers, unit administration, and school board
members
(*2*) Introductions of all attending
(*3*) Short talk by the community welcome wagon or chamber of commerce (with gifts)
(*4*) Short motivational talk by a local "teacher of the year" or teacher
organization president
(*5*) Facts and figures about the district
  • appreciation talk by superintendent and/or board president about
the teachers' hard work

(One district gives a bus tour of the district, pointing out buildings and
neighborhoods. This works well if you have many buildings and many
new teachers hired from outside your town. It would be silly if you had
eight new hires, all of whom already lived in a town of 15,000. Know
your teachers and plan the orientation with their needs. Your orientation
will be different each year, based on needs.)

  • begin specific district orientation if time permits
  • the school calendar, vacation days, open house dates, test dates
  • who to see for pay checks, help with finding housing, etc.

Lunch time—lunch on own so there is a little breathing time

Day 1—Afternoon session

(*1*) Orientation on district attendance, sick days, pay, benefits
(*2*) Background of legal issues that are specific to state and district
  • may include child abuse reporting and the issue of touching
children
(*3*) Where to get district-level help for students
  • special education help
  • guidance counseling
  • tutoring programs, before- and after-school day care

- meals and community welfare programs
- social workers and nurses
- media, library, and arts programs that are districtwide

(*4*) Explanation of mentor program, if program is districtwide

Day 2—Morning session
>   Where: held in each individual building
>   Taught by building principals and invited teachers

(*1*) Welcome and introduction to building-level administrators and support staff
(*2*) Facts and figures about the school
>   Hint: make this active learning. Pass out a mock test, let teachers answer and fill in the blanks so that they don't just sit and listen.
(*3*) The school day
- start time, dismissals, schedules
- special items, such as block scheduling, snow day schedules
- fire drill and emergency procedures

(*4*) Curricular issues
- buildings' school report card and explanation of required state and national tests
- overview of team teaching, reading and writing across the curriculum, and so forth

(*5*) How and where to get books and supplies
- explanation of how to request supplemental materials

(*6*) Orientation to the mentor program and how support is provided for new teachers
- clarification of the confidentiality factors of your mentor program
- clarification of mentoring vs. evaluation

Luncheon where new teachers meet their mentors!

Day 2—Afternoon to work with the mentor in classrooms
Teachers report that they need classroom work time more than anything else. However, some teachers may need guidance about how to work with their mentor in setting up their classroom. Your district's mentor training will address this issue.

- mentors will help new teacher find books, desks, and so on
- work with teacher with regard to curricular issues and "survival" skills, such as how to take lunch count and attendance.

Day 3—Morning meeting
Building level, presented by principals and department heads

(*1*) A follow-up about what the mentor can and cannot do for the new teacher

(*2*) Clarification of extracurricular duties, playground supervision, requests for teachers to serve on committees or as tutors, etc.

(*3*) Thorough explanation of how new teachers are evaluated for retention and tenure

(*4*) Explanation of staff development training opportunities available and/or required throughout the school year

(*5*) Session with the staff developer/university liaison who will teach the ongoing new teacher workshops throughout the year

Session on classroom management and discipline!

(*1*) Explanation of the school's policies on classroom management and discipline

(*2*) Creation of classroom posters by each teacher for their room
  • posters include rules, positives, and consequences

(*3*) Role-play scenarios that could really happen and what to do if they do!

Lunch provided by the teachers' association/union

Day 3—Afternoon spent with mentors in classrooms

(*1*) Mentors follow up on classroom management and discipline

(*2*) Some principals meet one-on-one with individuals during this time

After this new teacher orientation with work time in the classroom, the teachers will participate in the regular faculty back-to-school program. Chapter 12 on mentoring includes more specific activities to be completed by the mentor and the new teacher.

THE NOTEBOOK FOR NEW TEACHERS

Successful teachers are organized teachers and one way to help teachers to be organized from the beginning is to provide them a large looseleaf notebook for their handouts. Fill the notebook with the handouts for the orientation and whenever important handouts are given at the all-faculty meetings, pre-punch them so they are ready for the notebook. Will teachers be insulted by this practice? I don't think so. The dean of the college where I work makes notebooks for the faculty, all of whom have Ph.D.'s, and quite frankly, I have heard nothing but positive comments.

What goes into this notebook? How much time do new teachers (or any teachers) have to read notebooks? Are the teachers more apt to read materials generated by their peers? Do not make the notebook an encyclopedia. It is a reference, but it should be as short and concise as possible. It should be user friendly with a table of contents. It does not need to duplicate the student handbook or the teachers' union contract. Provide copies of the student handbook and contract with the notebook. Consider each of the following and decide if they should be included in your district's new teacher notebook.

Items for the notebook:

(*1*) Map of the town

(*2*) Directories of administrators, counselors, and support staff

(*3*) Directory of teaching personnel

(*4*) Calendar
  • include early release days, teacher workshop days
  • testing days, dates that grades are due
  • PAY DAYS!

(*5*) Schedules and policies
  • emergency preparedness, fire drills, snow days

(*6*) Copies of forms with note at bottom of each about when they are due and how to get more copies

(*7*) Blank forms for leaving a lesson plan for substitute (these should be filled out early in the school year and left in the upper-right hand drawer of teacher's desk)
  • the seating chart
  • a plan that can be used any day with this age student
  • at least three sponge activities to use with students

(*8*) A copy of the evaluation instrument used by principals and evaluators for formal observations

(*9*) Overview of classroom management expectations and/or district policies regarding discipline
  • excused vs. unexcused absences, suspension

(*10*) A glossary of abbreviations and definitions of special programs
  • REI, SRA, Chapter I, Carnegie Unit, TSS, CogAT, ITBS

Other Suggestions From School Districts

It is obvious that this type of notebook may become an encyclopedia! Some districts provide a small notebook and have each school provide one with the more specific items. One district provides the notebook with the policies and then provides a second booklet written by the teachers with the "survival skills." However your notebooks are arranged, be sure to include some motivational quotes from teachers in them. Any easy way to get quotes is to ask teachers to submit some. Again, the more teacher input in your guides and notebooks, the more they will be read and used.

QUESTIONS FOR DISCUSSION

(*1*) What does your district currently offer for new teacher orientation? Are there any topics or activities that have proven to be useful that are not listed in this chapter?

(*2*) How can you get the chamber of commerce or welcome wagon club to support new teachers?

(*3*) Can you pay the mentor teachers involved in orientation of new teachers? How much will this type of orientation cost your district? Where will the funds be found?

(*4*) Your district may not have three to five days for new teacher orientation. What is essential for a one-day orientation? Two days?

(*5*) All of the preparation needed to organize three days of orientation and to make a notebook and guidebook for new teachers is tremendous. As a busy personnel director or principal, how can you get help with these preparations?

(*6*) Ask districts for copies of their handbooks and orientation materials. Also ask if you may quote and reproduce specific items from their materials. Ask for copies of their new-teacher orientation. Compare these items to the suggestions in this chapter and then create your building and district orientation.

(*7*) This chapter has concentrated on orientation for new teachers. What does your district do to provide orientation for other new staff members, including custodians, secretaries, paraprofessionals, and administrators?

KEY POINTS

(*1*) Create user-friendly orientation sessions that take place in a comfortable, business-like environment.

(*2*) Use active learning strategies and variety in orientation presentations.

(*3*) Use teachers' input and evaluations for all orientation planning.

(*4*) Inform but do not overwhelm in new-teacher orientation.

CHAPTER 11

Support Seminars for Newly Hired Teachers

THE BEST ORIENTATION in the world is still just orientation. Some new teachers will be so overwhelmed by the amount of new information given in orientation that they cannot possibly absorb all of it. Others may be so stressed from finishing their degree program and moving into their first apartment that all of the details of their new school get lost in the shuffle of their other life experiences. Orientation is one part of staff development, and all staff development provides the best results when it is given in a timely manner, provided in a continual, ongoing framework. Orientation sets the stage for planned, systematic seminars that are provided for the new teachers throughout the school year. In fact, during the orientation inform new teachers about the dates of programs that will be offered to them during their initial year.

TIME FOR BEGINNING TEACHER PROGRAMS

In 1994 I visited New Zealand and had the opportunity to discuss induction and problems of new teachers with professors of higher education and beginning teachers themselves. The one most significant fact that I learned about being a first-year elementary teacher in New Zealand was that every new teacher was provided with a mentor and with 20% release time to work their mentor and/or pursue related staff development. A 20% release means *one day per week*. So, the new teacher would have up to one day per week to meet with the mentor teacher, observe in his/her classroom or have the mentor observe and team teach in the new teacher's classroom. The new teacher might use the one day a week to simply catch up on paperwork, lesson planning, and paper grading. He/she might use the time to return to the university for seminars or to visit another school to observe other teachers. Imagine the possibilities of one day a week preparing for teaching or working with a mentor to improve your professional practice! The students did not suffer because the school district hired a permanent substitute for each three to five new teachers hired. So, if a school hires a new teacher, they also hire a substitute who is available one day every week for that class. The substitute knows the students, the school, and the routines. The substitute may go into the mentor's room and teach there, allowing the mentor to work side-by-side with the new teacher.

The first-year teachers with whom I visited reported that they liked the support of their mentors (tutor teachers) and of their support seminars back at the university. In fact, one new teacher said that she could not imagine trying to do everything required of a veteran teacher without the release time for "catching up and getting organized." This same teacher indicated surprise that her U.S. counterparts did not receive the equivalent release time. She said, "Every beginner needs the release time. After all, we are still novices and are still learning. The school supports us. We can learn and teach and become established without being completely overwhelmed." If the New Zealand schools can provide one day a week of release time to support newly hired teachers, then your school district can provide at least some time for the ongoing support of new teachers. One day a month is a reasonable goal. Six days a year may be a minimum.

TYPES AND DELIVERY OF SUPPORT SEMINARS

The goals of support seminars for new teachers include providing ongoing training in teaching skills, further orientation to the school district and the teaching profession, and emotional support to the teacher. The philosophy behind the seminars should be one of providing the environment and/or relationship that the individual teachers may use for their own professional growth. In my article, *A Curriculum and Resources for Beginning Teacher Programs,* I wrote about psychologist Carl Rogers's philosophy toward his patients: "During his early professional years, Rogers (1961, p. 32) asked, "How can I treat, or cure, or change this person?" In time he learned to ask, "How can I provide a relationship which this person can use for his own professional growth?" (Clement, 1996, p. 87).

After spending so much time recruiting and hiring the best and the brightest, you do not need to treat, cure, or change your new teachers. You simply need to give them the supplies and space they need to work and the support they need to continue to grow! As one of my college professors used to say, "We are just like flowers. We all grow better with sunshine and water." The support seminars you create for your new teachers will be the sunshine and water they need to grow. Too often teachers isolate themselves in their classrooms and don't come out for any fresh air. Too much isolation causes burnout in the profession.

IMPORTANCE OF RELEASE TIME

The seminars for beginning teachers should be offered during release time. Teachers are too tired and too busy to work all day and then attend a seminar after school. In addition, most of the newly hired teachers may also be coaching a sport or sponsoring an after-school activity. Plan for a minimum of six days of release time for the new teachers to meet for their seminars. I worked with the Mattoon, Illinois, school district for six years as they implemented a model beginning teacher program. All newly hired teachers were provided with a list of the seminar dates during orientation. The seminars were held one day a month in August/September, October, November, February, March, and April. The secondary teachers were released to meet in the mornings because so many of them had afternoon coaching and extracurricular duties that began early in the afternoon. The elementary teachers were released in the afternoons, and their evaluations told us that they preferred to be in their classrooms in the mornings for all-important reading and language arts instruction. This district was able to share the substitutes that were hired, switching them from secondary to elementary assignments as the day progressed. Yes, the scheduling was tricky, but the system worked well for this school district with twenty to forty new hires a year. A few teachers indicated that as new teachers they did not like to leave their classes to a substitute, and as worthwhile as they found the seminars, they would have preferred to meet after school, but the vast majority said the release time for seminars was fantastic.

If release time is impossible for the new teachers, try other options. I have also taught seminars that were offered after school and in the evenings. One successful evening program was offered by a regional office of education for beginning teachers. This office allowed time for the teachers to leave school and run errands or start the family's evening, then meet as a group from 5:30 to 9:00 P.M., with dinner included. Since the group met only six times throughout the school year, the teachers could plan ahead for the meetings. All the teachers "talked shop" and shared ideas throughout the dinner as well. Twice I was asked to teach Saturday seminars for beginning teachers. Again, the teachers who attended rated the seminars very highly and said that they learned much from the seminars and felt much support by being able to talk with their colleagues away from their school buildings and administrators. However, several teachers who attended the voluntary evening and Saturday programs said that the new teachers who were really struggling did not attend the sessions. (Much as teachers complain that only the best parents attend the parent conferences!)

If your district is implementing a new program, survey the participants or survey new employees from the past two years to see if they prefer after-school, evening, Saturday, or release-time programs. As with orientation, provide refreshments and make sure the meeting room is convenient and comfortable. Above all, make sure that the curriculum is relevant and that much time is devoted at every session for the teachers to share their joys and concerns. After all, a main goal is to alleviate isolation, so the teachers need time and a venue to talk with other teachers. You will know that the sessions are going well if the teachers do more talking that the presenter/facilitator and if the teachers report feeling that they are not alone in trying to survive their first year.

WHO SHOULD SERVE AS THE LEADER/PRESENTER/FACILITATOR?

For six years I served as the director of a university's beginning teacher program. All of my teaching was off-campus. In fact, my job was to assist school districts to develop their programs for new teachers and then to teach the seminars we developed. If there is a university near your district, find out if they offer this type of outreach and service to school districts. An advantage in having an "outsider" lead the seminars is that confidentiality of problems can be maintained and that there is no conflict between helping the new teacher with problems and evaluation of the new teacher. I was not a part of any district's gossip grapevine, nor did I have a part in the hiring or evaluation of any of the new teachers.

Finding a university to supply a professor with the time and background needed to lead your district's program may not be possible. Using internal administrators and veteran teachers as the leaders/presenters has many advantages. People within your district know the system and its policies. Many times the curriculum director, personnel director, or assistant superintendent organizes and teaches the sessions. In other school districts one principal may provide the seminars for all new teachers in the districts, or the sessions may be designed and taught by veteran teachers. A successful presenter will have knowledge of the problems of new teachers, have patience and compassion for the new teachers, and have a genuine interest in promoting improved teaching. The leaders have to model good teaching—being organized and flexible. They have to understand the confidentiality factors involved, since many of the seminars may include discussion of problems and concerns.

CURRICULAR ISSUES

Designing curriculum for beginning teacher programs is easy. Simply refer to the problems beginning teachers encounter and allow sessions for each of the problems! If you want to approach the curriculum from a total constructivist point of view, then allow the teachers to brainstorm at the first session about what they want to be included in the sessions and design the sessions from their concerns. When I began teaching seminars, I surveyed a group of fifty-five beginning teachers about topics that would interest them enough that they would *attend* the seminars. They wanted to attend sessions dealing with effective teaching techniques for their specific grade levels and subject areas, behavior management and discipline, grading and evaluation, individual differences, and students' emotional and substance abuse problems. In addition, they wanted sessions dealing with stress management. In most of my seminar series, I am also able to allow time to address specific topics that develop. For example, in one of the Saturday programs, most of the first-year teachers were going to change jobs at the end of their first year and requested a seminar on resumé writing and interviewing for our last session. While I hadn't thought of this as a possible topic, once it was included on the schedule, it received the highest ratings from this group of teachers. It met a very immediate need for them.

SEMINAR 1—GETTING STARTED, GETTING ORGANIZED

The curriculum that has served as a base for my programs for beginning teachers follows the patterns of needs of teachers through a school year. Our initial seminar is titled, "A New Beginning" or "Getting Started, Getting Organized." At this initial seminar it is vitally important to allow time for the teachers to get to know each other and for the presenter to get to know the teachers' backgrounds and needs. The presenter should stress the importance of the teachers getting to know their students in the same way. I have often used interest inventories designed for students with the new teachers. I ask them to complete the survey with their own interests first and then to complete the survey as if they were one of their students. As a follow-up, I recommend that they give the survey to their new students and compare the answers with what they thought they would say. Teachers who do not even begin to know the favorite band or TV show of their students should get to know their interests if they plan to survive in the classroom! Time should be spent with introductions and easy get-acquainted activities. Then, discussions of how to organize the classroom can take place. Activities regarding grading and classroom management are a must, but keep these activities short and simple. It is very important to share resources at the initial meeting. The resources include district ones, such as where the teachers' resources can be found, as well as sharing copies of magazines and books for the new teachers.

Always end the first session with an inspirational thought or poem. Now is the time to be upbeat and positive. Celebrate the success that these teachers have found their first job and are getting started in their own classrooms. (Sample lesson plans, activities, and discussion questions are listed for each of the six seminars discussed. Resources are included too.)

Lesson Ideas for Seminar 1

Getting Started, Getting Organized

(1) Introductions: Have teachers introduce themselves with their name, school location, grade/subject levels, and what they are looking forward to the most. Remind the group that they must remember what each teacher teaches, as the next activity involves that knowledge.

Then, do the introductions again, but this time the teachers introduce themselves as they will on the first day of class to their students.

- remind teachers of using titles, as they want the students to address them

(2) The alphabet activity: Have teachers form pairs. Assign a letter of the alphabet to each pair. The pair will write something about that letter that relates to teaching. Obviously, some pairs may do several letters. After a short time (three minutes) have teachers read their teacher's alphabet.

Example: C is for computers—we all need one in our classrooms. P is for paperwork—how can we possibly handle it all?

(3) The survival guide: Form groups of three teachers. Each group should think of a rule they would create for surviving during the first year of teaching (or in a new job in a new school). The groups will then present their rule and the others will guess the rule. Ask the group, "How can you present new material?" They will answer with "by lecturing," "by a poster," "through a role-play," and so on. Have the group present their rule in these ways. Encourage role-plays, singing, and other interesting ways of presenting their rule. Make a list of the rules, advice, and ideas presented. Sample rules might include:

(*1*) Know when to go home. You can't live at school.
(*2*) Exercise to get more energy.
(*3*) Talk with your mentor.
(*4*) Talk with your colleagues.
(*5*) Creativity is a good thing, but you can borrow ideas and worksheets, too.
(*6*) Remember you teach little human beings, not just a subject.
(*7*) Teachers have to be flexible, very flexible.
(*8*) Always have a Plan B since you never know when half of your class will be called out for hearing tests.
(*9*) Get organized about paperwork and get it turned in on time.
(*10*) Remember to say kind words. Words go straight from your mouth to the ears of parents at home.
(*11*) Act like a professional. You are one!
(*12*) Be kind to yourself. Reward yourself in positive ways for your hard work.

(4) The interest inventory: Make a handout using these following sentence starters. Most teachers will want two, one to write on and one to take back and use with their students. These are general

questions. Many examples of premade inventories can be found in the Lee Canter materials.

(*1*) The one thing I like the most about school is . . .
(2) My very favorite TV show is . . .
(*3*) Some day I want to be a . . .
(*4*) If I were a movie star, I would want to be . . .
(*5*) When I have free time, I like to . . .
(*6*) If I could travel anywhere, I would want to go to . . .
(*7*) My favorite music is . . .
(*8*) I would really like to meet (fill in a famous person's name). . . because . . .

Share some examples of what the teachers write about themselves and about what they think their students will say. Share other interest inventories and ones that are specific to school subjects and knowledge of subject matter. Encourage teachers to write ones for their grade/subject.

(5) The organizing activity: Put the following questions on the board or overhead to get the teachers to brainstorm about the best ways to organize their new classroom.

(*1*) As the students enter I need for them to . . .
(2) Students can always pick up graded papers at . . .
(*3*) Students can always turn in papers at . . .
(*4*) Make-up work will always be posted or printed at . . .
(*5*) The bathroom pass policy will be . . .
(*6*) The dismissal policy will be . . .
(*7*) My signals for quiet will be . . .
(*8*) The policies for transitions (whole group to small group, one group leaves for special activity, etc.) will be . . .

After brainstorming teach some of the following:

(*1*) Always have a way for students to enter the room. An excellent entrance is for them to pass by your entrance table, which has graded papers in folders with their names on them, workbooks, and any other materials needed for that class. Students know to pick up what they need, get seated and then look at the board for the first assignment of the day.
(2) Keep an outline of your plan on the board or overhead so students know what to do and why it's important.

(*3*) Provide materials for teachers to make seating charts. Materials include heavy paper, post-it notes, and sheet protectors. Show a sample of writing each student's name on a post-it note, then arranging them on the heavy paper. A vinyl sheet protector then covers the paper so that teacher can write notes about absences or grades with an overhead marker pen. If students need to be moved, just lift the sheet protector, move the post-it note, and the seating chart can be used all year!

(6) The classroom management activity: Have teachers write three to five rules that will be the classroom rules in their room. Review school and district policies that may exist. Then, have one group of teachers teach their rules and the consequences to the group as if we were their students.

Have other teachers explain their rules to the group as if we were parents at an open house, then parents in a conference. Have a third group explain their rules and consequences to the group as if the group were the principal. Many districts have teachers make posters for their room at this meeting.

(7) The grading activity: Again, pair teachers. Have each teacher explain to his/her partner how his/her grading system works. Have the other teacher play the parent or principal, asking the type of questions that a parent or principal would ask.

Note: Every time I have done this activity with new teachers, there have been teachers who did not know how to set up a grading scale. They were not required to do this in student teaching or field experience. I always keep some extra handouts with ideas for grading for these teachers. Often the other teacher in the pair will share usable ideas. As the presenter, be ready for teachers who may not want to set up any system for grading or for any classroom rules.

(8) If time permits, have teachers discuss how to leave plans for a substitute and also have teachers share their best idea for sponge activities. (Sponge activities are little time fillers that work well when the teacher sees that students are done and there are extra minutes of time to fill!)

This will more than fill your first seminar! The point for this and future seminars is to involve teachers actively and to use their shared knowledge. Remember to end with a positive and send the teachers out feeling confident and ready! The following anonymous poem is one I often read:

> I teach because I see the hope
> an education brings,
> Because the treasures found in books
> give children stronger wings.
> I can't replace the parents
> of those I see each day,
> But I can teach, and gently coax,
> young hearts who come my way.

Resources: *Teaching k-8, Learning, Instructor* magazines
Kappa Delta Pi's *New Teacher Advocate* and *Record*
Harry Wong's *The First Days of School: How to Be an Effective Teacher.*

SEMINAR 2—COMMUNICATING WITH PARENTS, COLLEAGUES, ADMINISTRATORS, AND EVEN THE STUDENTS

Plan to schedule this seminar about two weeks before the teachers are expected to meet parents and conduct parent conferences. Very few student teachers are involved in parent conferencing, and even if they were, they are often hesitant about conducting their own. The teachers need to be presented with information about how to talk with parents and with specific guidelines for conducting the conferences. As I have outlined in the lesson ideas, the teachers need to practice how they will talk to parents in role-play and practice scenarios. Since many teachers are themselves parents, let teachers share the best and maybe even the worst communications that they have had with parents.

At this session, review any school policy and procedures necessary. For example, I used to teach at a school that held parent conferences in the evenings. This may cause concerns about commuting or finding a baby-sitter for the teachers and they need to know as early as possible exactly what hours are required of them. Some schools now conduct parent conferences at tables in the cafeteria and gym, since there were concerns about teacher safety if the teacher met parents one-on-one in the classroom.

End this seminar by asking teachers about classroom management concerns and use their input for the next seminar.

Lesson Ideas for Seminar 2

Communicating with parents, colleagues, administrators,
and even students

(1) As a warm-up, have teachers reintroduce themselves by telling the best thing that has happened in their classroom since the first seminar.

(2) To focus on the topic of parent communication, have teachers share the best examples that they know for teachers reaching out to parents. Hint: Have some examples ready in case the teachers don't have any!

(3) Teach the golden rule of parent communication: Treat parents the way that you would want your child's teacher to treat you. Ask the group scenario questions and then ask them to discuss if this merits a communication with a parent. If it does, what type of communication might be best, a call, a note, or a request for a conference? Examples:

(*1*) Susan cheated on a chapter test. Should parents be informed?

(*2*) Dale was caught stealing candy from another student's desk.

(*3*) Terry was caught smoking in the restroom.

(*4*) Mindy announces that her mom hit her this morning.

(*5*) Bill has not turned in any homework for a week.

(*6*) You feel that Teresa is not bringing her glasses to school because other students make fun of her when she wears them.

(*7*) Jerome has been using profanity incessantly.

(*8*) Heidi has the mumps and will be out of school a week.

(*9*) Marty just scored the winning touchdown at the homecoming game.

(*10*) Amanda received her first A in your class.

(4) Show samples of notes and newsletters sent home. Explain what constitutes a good example.

(5) Teach the easy way to call a parent.

(*1*) Get a notecard.

(*2*) Write out how you will introduce yourself. "Hi, I'm Mrs. Clement, John's Spanish teacher."

(*3*) Find out with whom you are speaking, and if that person is the appropriate caregiver with whom you can share information.

(*4*) State why you are calling (to introduce yourself, to inform parent of a concern or behavior, to share good news, etc.).

(*5*) If you are calling about a problem, state a solution.

(*6*) Get some parent input or response.

(*7*) Have a quick way to get off the phone.

(*8*) Date and keep the card in your files.

Have teachers practice calling irate parents. Role-plays are great here.

(6) Explain the importance of a parent conference and have the teachers generate a list of "what to do for a successful parent conference." Hints:

(*1*) Welcome the parent as if you were an executive in a big company. Always stand up and shake hands. Offer an ADULT-SIZED chair.

(2) Sit at a table with the parents, not behind your desk.

(3) Show examples of student's work from a folder.

(4) Start and end with a positive.

(5) If you and the parent work out a tutoring plan or other special arrangement, remember to follow through with the plan.

(6) If a parent becomes belligerent or seems to be intoxicated, get back-up support from another teacher or administrator.

(7) Always talk about behaviors. Example: Marty does not turn in homework regularly. Let's look at the specific cases of missing papers. Not: Marty is careless and lazy about homework.

Then have teachers write possible scenarios that they expect to come up in conferences. Role-play the scenarios so that the new teachers start to feel confident and prepared for upcoming conferences.

(7) Discuss good communication with colleagues. This is the perfect time to remind the teachers about what their mentors can and cannot do for them. Mentors are their front-line colleagues when questions and problems arise. Many beginning teachers express feelings of concern about veteran teachers criticizing them. Seminars are a good time to discuss the veteran-rookie relationships and the politics of the ubiquitous teachers' lounge.

(8) Discuss communication with administrators. Have new teachers been observed by the administrators yet? Do they understand the evaluation process?

(9) Share teachers' ideas for improved communication with students regarding make-up work, lost assignments, and so on. Wrap up!

SEMINAR 3—APPROACHES TO CLASSROOM MANAGEMENT

While it may seem to some that the third seminar is a bit late for the topic of classroom management and discipline, I have found the topic to be well received at this time. By the end of the first grading quarter, new teachers may want to update their rules and procedures and want help in doing so. Many new teachers, in spite of college training about management and in spite of the mini-workshop on management at the first seminar, still do not create a workable classroom management plan. New teachers often start out "too easy" and have great difficulty managing their classes after the honeymoon phase of the beginning of the school year.

I always remind teachers that today's students need parameters for their behavior and that parents and administrators expect appropriate parameters to be set. Students and parents want their classrooms to be safe environments where learning takes place. Good classroom management does not just happen—teachers have to plan for it.

The lesson ideas for this seminar include presenting the materials that are available by Lee Canter and others, and getting the teachers to evaluate which classroom management strategies will work best for them. Again, role-plays can be very helpful. Allowing the teachers to write specific questions and then getting the others to help answer the questions makes this seminar very real to all participants.

Lesson Ideas for Seminar 3

Approaches to Classroom Management

(1) Focus the group by asking about positive parent communications that have occurred since the second seminar.

(2) Get input from teachers about the district plan, the school plan, and their classroom plans for classroom management and discipline.

(3) Present a synopsis of Lee Canter's materials for classroom management.

(*1*) Include interest inventories, getting to know students, and reaching out to parents.

(*2*) Discuss briefly the old "assertive discipline" and explain why names and checks on the chalkboard probably doesn't work. Remind students of how the Canter materials have been updated in the 1990s.

(*3*) Present strategies from Canter's *Succeeding with Difficult Students.*

(*4*) Present ideas from Canter's *Behavior Management in the Middle School.*

Note: If possible, have the district provide copies of the Canter materials to teachers. If individual copies aren't possible, copies can be available in a resource library. I often bring several copies of *Succeeding with Difficult Students* to a seminar and have teachers read parts from the scenarios in the book. As the teachers hear themselves reading the part of nonassertive or hostile teacher they realize how ineffective those behaviors are in the classroom.

(4) Present a synopsis of ideas from Harry Wong's *The First Days of Schools: How to Be an Effective Teacher.*
- Discuss how a routine is different from a rule
- Discuss rewards and consequences
- Discuss high expectations and how to teach children those expectations
- Discuss ways to get administrative support

(5) Present other authors and their ideas on classroom management and discipline. Share titles that are useful and ordering information or information about which books are already in the library. I often use Carol Fuery Ruot's *Discipline Strategies for the Bored, Belligerent, and Ballistic in Your Classroom* as another resource.

(6) After the presentation and review of current practices in management and discipline, have teachers write a specific question or problem on a notecard. As a presenter, read these problems and questions and have small groups work together to help answer and solve some of the problems. Questions and problems brought up in past seminars include:

(*1*) Two seventh-grade girls will not be quiet. I have tried separating them, giving detentions, and every other strategy I can think of. How do I get them to be quiet?

(*2*) Kyle came into class yesterday, threw his books on his desk, and said in his rudest voice, "I hate this school. I hate this class and I hate you, too." What should I have done?

(*3*) Tardies and absences are my biggest discipline problem. How do I get kids to school on time?

(*4*) I have a class of twenty-five students in which about ten do not care whether they pass or not. These ten talk and goof off constantly. I can't just send ten to the office. What do I do?

(*5*) I have students who whine all the time. They are chronic complainers. Do I discipline for this?

(*6*) I use parent calls and parent conferences as "consequences" in my management plan. Yet, I often cannot reach parents or they will not come in for a conference. What should I do?

(*7*) Two second-graders in my class are wanderers—they just will not stay in their seats. Any suggestions?

(*8*) I want to be creative and group students at tables, but that arrangement leads to so much noise. Is it alright to use rows in elementary classes?

(*9*) Three or four of my students talk back to me and contest what I say. How can I stop this verbal fighting with my students?

(*10*) I have several students who rush through their work doing a terrible job, then sit at their desks and say, "We're bored. This class is dumb." Is this a discipline problem and what do I do?

Teachers will write incredible and true examples. Let them do so and allow time for solutions.

(7) Role-play scenarios of how the teacher should sound and exactly what he/she should say in challenging situations. Stress lowering the voice, never yelling. Remind teachers that eye contact and proximity are good for defusing some situations, but that angry students become worse if the teacher is too close or "in their face." Discuss cultural differences and how some students may want more space when confronted.

Note: Many teachers tell me that role-plays have helped them tremendously, as they did not know what to say in certain situations, especially when confronted by an irate student. Teachers often laugh in the role-plays, but they do help them.

(8) Discuss the teachers' feelings of being "mean" and being "nice." Applying classroom management and discipline does not make a teacher mean, although many teachers express this feeling. Discussions of being the friend and buddy may also develop in this seminar.

(9) Wrap up with something very positive. Provide as many books and resources about management to the teachers as possible. Get their input about a follow-up seminar on this topic. Often I allow time at each of the future seminars to follow up on the management issues.

SEMINAR 4—DEALING WITH STUDENTS' SOCIAL AND EMOTIONAL PROBLEMS; ALSO GIFTED, INCLUSION, AND SPECIAL EDUCATION

So often the dialogue in the teachers' lounge centers on "bad" kids and why they are driving their teachers crazy. The truth is that today's teachers are asked to teach all students and that the diversity of students in our classrooms is greater than ever before. This is a challenge, but discussing students' problems, their diversity, and their specialness can help teachers to face the challenges and deal effectively with their students. This seminar provides a good opportunity for teachers to work together with the other teachers, counselors, psychologists, and consultants who are available to help the classroom teachers with students. Let teachers know that others are there to help them, and provide books and magazine articles with specific hints on dealing with today's students.

This seminar routinely occurs when teachers may be depressed about student achievement in general, especially the achievement of special needs students. This seminar can include materials about motivating all students—and motivating the teachers! It is timely that this seminar follows the one on classroom management and discipline, since the two are so closely related. Our special needs students may also be a cause of our classroom discipline challenges. Again, devoting time to discuss these concerns and providing some outside speakers and resources at this point in the new teachers' school year will provide some much-needed support.

Ideas for Seminar 4

Dealing with Students' Social and Emotional Problems,
Gifted, Inclusion, and Special Education

(1) A focus activity: Ask teachers to describe the students in their classes. Perhaps they can even write for a few minutes describing individual students. You may want to have half of the teachers write about their top students and half of the group write about their at-risk students. Since teachers know each other's students, make the standard disclaimer that we are doing this activity as a way to better teach *all* students. Ask teachers to change names. You may want them to write about their students, then share without any names. As teachers describe students, start a list of adjectives on the board describing these students. Call the list "today's students." Here's a sample of what teachers often say or write to describe their students:

- loud, rude, noisy
- needing attention
- very social and talkative
- talented and eager to learn, especially arts and technology
- very advanced socially (much more aware of the world than we were at their age)
- streetwise
- savvy in the ways of the world and how to get their way
- manipulative
- hungry and poorly clothed
- wealthy and better dressed than the teachers

One teacher answered this activity by saying that her students were overexposed to the negatives in life, but underexposed to the positives.

The idea of this focus activity is to get the teachers to think about the diversity of their students as a way to begin to meet their needs. After the descriptions appear on the chalkboard, ask these questions:

(*1*) Do the students you teach have stress in their lives?
(2) Do the students have real problems?

(*3*) What can you do to meet their needs?
(*4*) Now, how can we work to meet their academic needs?

The discussion of how to help students is important. Many new teachers begin to feel that they cannot teach the students in their classrooms because of all the social and emotional problems that the students bring with them to school. We've all heard of psychologists refering to this as "emotional baggage." This is an excellent time for the district's social workers, guidance counselors, and school psychologists to make presentations to the new teachers. It is good to review the programs that are already in place for helping students in the district. Topics for this seminar include:

- dealing with children's anger and stress
- helping children to learn about their feelings
- dealing with substance abuse and alcoholism
- helping children of alcoholics to cope and succeed in school
- helping children from abusive home backgrounds
- helping students cope with divorce in the family
- helping students accept racial diversity and fight prejudices

Teachers may want to discuss ways to incorporate life themes into class assignments, such as journal writing. There are many ways to help the students in our classes to overcome difficult life situations and to succeed. It has often been said that one caring teacher can make the difference in a student being "at risk" or "at promise."

(2) The second part of this seminar can deal with gifted education and special education. Again, it is a good idea to bring in speakers from these departments in the district. Representatives from these areas probably met with the new teachers at the orientation, but later in the year teachers will have many more questions.

If no time can be alloted for specialists to present, the regular presenter can share best ideas and strategies. It is always good to begin the discussion by asking the teachers some ways that they are addressing the special needs of the students in their classes. Many teachers are already using good ideas that they can share. Ask questions to begin the discussion:

- How do you deal with the brainchild who is always miles ahead of others and who is always finished with work ahead of his/her peers?

- Do you ever feel that your most advanced students may be learning the least because the rest of the class is holding them back and you simply end up "teaching to the middle?"
- Do you worry that your brightest students really are bored?

Ideas for this seminar can be found in Susan Winebrenner's *Teaching Gifted Kids in the Regular Classroom*.

(3) Special education and inclusion are always hot topics for beginning teachers. The teachers may want to discuss working with special education teachers before any of them come to present at the seminar, so that their discussion may be frank and open. Or, they may need to have their frank and open discussion with the special education teachers! There are many, many resources available on this topic. One general source is Susan Winebrenner's *Teaching Kids With Learning Difficulties in the Regular Classroom*.

SEMINAR 5—TEACHING STRATEGIES

Even outstanding new teachers may be feeling that they have run out of ideas by mid-term of the second semester. The teaching strategies seminar can address strategies, tricks, and teaching hints through discussions of what is new and what is working by grade and subject areas. As teachers relate their "best practices," they also address the question, "Are students learning what we are teaching and how do we know?"

It is only after teachers have survived the first semester that they feel more confident and are ready to try some new strategies. Reviewing the benefits of cooperative group work, integrating technology, and hands-on activities will encourage teachers to make changes and keep students actively engaged.

Again, the seminar is the time to share more resources. Teachers always like free samples of magazines and journals. Bring the media specialist to this session, as well as the district curriculum director and/or reading specialists to share new ideas. Inviting the regional Office of Education consultants to share about a "hot topic" will encourage the teachers to not only consider the innovation shared, but will also make the new teachers aware of outside resources available to them.

Above all, let the teachers themselves share their ideas. New teachers do not have to re-invent the wheel, but they do need to individualize even the best ideas for their own classrooms. Make sure that each teacher leaves this session with a least one new idea to try out immediately in his/her classroom. In fact, this is a good review for the seminar—asking each teacher present which idea or suggestion they will try first! Be sure to remind teachers that they can also review material by having students report what they learned during that class.

Lesson Ideas for Seminar 5

Teaching Strategies

(1) Focus activity: Put the following questions on the overhead to begin discussions:

(*1*) The best techniques for settling my class and starting the lesson are . . .

(*2*) One of my best activities for students to do in pairs is . . .

(*3*) We use the computers for . . .

(*4*) We use the Internet when we . . .

(*5*) Our best cooperative learning activity this year has been . . .

(*6*) A good review for student is . . .

(*7*) One of my best writing activities is . . .

(*8*) One of my best listening activities is . . .

(*9*) We use supplemental books for . . .

(*10*) A good outdoor experiential education activity for my class is . . .

(*11*) The students really learn new material well when I . . .

(*12*) The students report that their favorite activities are . . .

Depending on the size of the group, have teachers discuss their answers as a whole group or in small groups, based on grade and/or subject level.

(2) Lesson-planning activity: Pair teachers by grade and/or subject levels as closely as possible. Ask teachers to write down a topic or concept that they plan to teach within the next week. Then, have them discuss ways to present the new material or concept, to get students to practice with the new material, and ways to assess the students' understanding.

(3) Do a cooperative group activity that models how to set up groups, how to name a recorder, and so on. Pose a challenging

question such as, "If your school received a million dollars tomorrow, and your group got to decide where the money would be spent, how would you spend it?" Get groups to answer, then challenge them to come up with follow-up writing activities that would make this question an interdisciplinary one. Next, ask the teachers to write at least three questions that they could pose to their students to be answered in this way. (Many teachers have told me that they like this activity so well that they intend to use it routinely with *their* students.)

(4) Since this seminar deals with teaching strategies, it may also work well to deal with the issues of assessment, grading, and promotion at this time. Nothing generates debate as much as grading and assessment! Ask teachers about their concerns and about grade inflation to begin discussions. Also, discuss portfolio assessment.

As usual, this seminar could easily be turned into more than one!

SEMINAR 6—STRESS MANAGEMENT

As with the other topics, some teachers may say that the last seminar is too late for stress management. They have been stressed all year! I generally incorporated a stress buster or motivational segment in each of the seminars, then devoted the last one to this topic. The stress of successfully winding up a school year can be great for all teachers, and particularly overwhelming for beginners.

The key to teaching about stress management is to emphasize that everyone has stress, and that everyone must find their own solutions to solving their specific stressors. We must know what causes our stress before we can address it and do something about it. I use personal examples when I teach this seminar. For example, I recognize that gardening is a stress reliever for many people, but if I had to garden it would cause me great stress. I realized long ago that I could not manage my career and have a Martha Stewart-perfect house at the same time. My great husband does more of the housework now—and I have to accept that he does it on his time and in his own way.

With regard to the specific stressors caused by the teaching profession, we have to find ways to grow and learn about the problems we encounter in teaching so that we can resolve them. I often end this seminar by reminding teachers of the quote, "Grant me the patience to accept the things I cannot change, the courage to change the things I can, and the wisdom to know the difference." Many resource materials about stress management can be found at any bookstore. I have found some great articles in popular magazines at the supermarket check-out counter.

I have mentioned before that we should always celebrate the successes of the beginning teachers. This is especially true at the last seminar. Talk with the teachers about the importance of professionalism as well. Encourage them to think about a summer course to learn more new ideas, or start a discussion about continuing their education to earn a master's degree. Have the teachers complete evaluations of the seminars and enlist their support to help present at next year's seminars. Use the input that the teachers provide to gain support for the program to continue. End on a positive note and wish everyone a good ending to their first year of teaching. Good or bad, it is a year that no teacher ever forgets.

Lesson Ideas for Seminar 6

Stress Management

(1) Focus activity: Have teachers take a stress test. Many such tests exist. One example can be found in Billie Enz' *Teacher's Toolbox: A Primer for New Professionals*. The stress test that I developed and have used is included in this section. It may be used for the focus activity.

Stress Test: The ABC's of Stress Management

Where are the problems? On a scale of 1 to 10, where 1 is no stress and 10 is high stress, rate the following teaching concerns:

(*1*) Communicating and dealing with parents. _____

(*2*) Communicating and dealing with colleagues. _____

(*3*) Communicating and dealing with administrators. _____

(*4*) Presenting and teaching subject material. _____

(*5*) Classroom management and discipline. _____

(*6*) Dealing with inclusion/special education students. _____

(*7*) Too many students in my class(es). _____

(*8*) Physical classroom—size, heat, cleanliness. _____

(*9*) Motivating students to do their work/learn. _____

(*10*) Not having enough materials/supplies/books. _____

(*11*) Grading the students' work/assigning grades. _____

(*12*) Dealing with the students' social and emotional problems. _____

(*13*) Dealing with students' substance abuse problems. _____

(*14*) Dealing with criticism from the public/community about my job. _____

(*15*) Not enough time in the day to actually teach my classes. _____

(*16*) Tenure/employment next year. _____

Now do the same type of ratings on some personal questions.

(*1*) Not enough time to be with my family/spouse. _____

(*2*) Not enough time to socialize with friends. _____

(*3*) Not enough time for me to relax and do nothing. _____

(*4*) Not enough time to spend with my children. _____

(*5*) Dealing with aging parents or in-laws. _____

(*6*) Money and financial concerns. _____

(*7*) My own health problems. _____

(*8*) Health problems of immediate family members. _____

(*9*) Household cooking, cleaning, chores, and laundry. _____

(*10*) Don't like the area and/or climate and weather where we live. _____

After taking this stress test, list the items which you gave a 6 or higher. Now, what can you do about this concern? For example, if dealing with students' social and emotional problems is giving you great stress, can you attend a seminar on just this topic? Can you work with the counselors at your school and start a plan to rotate two students per week out to get some counseling?

(2) After the focus activity, the presenter will discuss the facts about stress. Stress is everywhere. In fact, it's called the disease of our times. We can lower our stress to a workable level by assessing what is actually causing the stress and then finding individual solutions to the stressors.

(3) Brainstorm with the teachers about positive stress relievers, such as exercise and support groups. Lots of PE and health teachers will gladly share ideas with the teachers in this seminar.

(4) After working out the problems of teachers' stress, there should be discussion of student stress and how we can help our

students to overcome stress. Conflict management is also a requested topic for this seminar.

(5) Since this seminar is often the last in the series, plan time for summarizing the year. Ask teachers to reflect upon the year with discussion questions such as:

(1) The most important thing I learned this year was . . .
(2) Next year I know that I will change the following . . .
(3) If I were starting the year over again, I would . . .
(4) I will be better organized next year by . . .
(5) I want to be the kind of teacher who . . .

(6) Teachers may need some specific ideas for activities that will help them to wrap up the year with students. Have veterans share their best ideas and also have one or two mentors come to the last session to share the specific policies on turning in the last grades, taking care of keys, and so forth.

(7) Last of all, celebrate the successes and encourage the teachers to rejuvenate over the summer and return fresh and motivated in August!

Evaluate the program and the seminars at the last session. Use the evaluations to improve the new teacher seminars for the next year.

DISCUSSION QUESTIONS

(1) Are there special curricular topics that need to be addressed in your district? Will you need a session for new teachers about state-mandated goals and testing? Will you need an entire seminar devoted to student diversity or preventing violence?

(2) Can your district work with a nearby university to provide graduate credit to the teachers for attending these sessions? Can teachers receive any continuing education/staff development hours toward continued certification?

(3) How will you handle a new teacher who does not attend these seminars? If a teacher is extremely reluctant to leave his/her class with a substitute, is this a cause for concern?

(4) How can you encourage veteran teachers on your staff to share their best teaching ideas with the new teachers?

(*5*) Many parents want their child to be taught by the regular classroom teacher every day. If a parent complains about the new teacher being out of the class six days for this program, how would you defend the release time?

KEY POINTS

(*1*) Provide time for support seminars throughout the school year and create a comfortable environment for the meetings.
(*2*) The leader and seminar presenters should be carefully chosen for their patience with new teachers, teaching skills, and staff development skills.
(*3*) The curriculum should be practical—providing help with organizational strategies, communication, and management skills.
(*4*) Always allow time for the teachers to talk about their joys and concerns. This opportunity provides much of the "support" discussed.
(*5*) Include help for working with special education, inclusion, and gifted students.
(*6*) Let teachers celebrate their successes!

CHAPTER 12

Mentoring

CELEBRITIES AND POLITICIANS proclaim the advantages of mentoring young people. Young executives seek mentors in order to "break through" to the top jobs. Even the hit television comedy "Seinfeld" had an episode about mentoring. Mentoring is a hot topic because of the potential for growth when a beginner is paired with a veteran who can serve as a guide, role model, friend, confidante, and even teacher to the novice. In a school district, a mentor program can be a powerful tool in supporting new faculty while helping to reward and rejuvenate veteran faculty.

Because of the popularity of mentoring, more school districts probably have some type of mentoring program than have release-time seminars for their newly hired teachers. Many states have mandated programs for the mentoring of new teachers (Huling-Austin et al., 1989). Mandated or not, mentoring programs may take a variety of forms. In many districts the mentors serve as volunteers to work one-on-one with new teachers as their time and teaching schedules permit. Some districts release veteran teachers for specific amounts of time during the day to work as mentors. In other districts the veteran teacher is released from classroom duties for one to three years in order to mentor as many as a dozen new teachers. A district may create a position or group of positions so that the mentors are full-time staff developers. Some districts have successfully experimented with hiring recently retired teachers to return for a few hours a week to mentor new teachers. The "veteran" mentor does not necessarily have to be an "old" veteran of many decades of teaching. In one of the programs that I worked, several newly hired teachers expressed gratitude for being paired with other young teachers who had just survived their first or second year. They felt that the "recent rookies" could relate well to the problems of being alone in a new community, renting the first apartment, making financial ends meet, and knowing what it felt like to be a beginner.

GUIDELINES FOR ESTABLISHING YOUR PROGRAM

An effective mentoring program does not simply happen because a school or district sees the need for it. Much thought needs to go into the planning of the program—planning for the goals, personnel, training of mentors, follow-up, and program evaluation. In other words, plan to answer these questions:

(*1*) What is the philosophy behind our program and what are our goals?
(*2*) Who will lead the program, from establishing it to making it permanent in our district?
(*3*) What will the costs be and how will the program be funded?
(*4*) Who will serve as mentors and how will they be selected?
(*5*) How will mentors be trained in their roles and responsibilities?
(*6*) How will we contact the new teachers and how will new hires be paired with the mentors?
(*7*) What kind of follow-up will be needed throughout the year to support the mentors?
(*8*) How will we assess the effectiveness of the program?
(*9*) Should the mentoring be extended to help the teachers in their second year or beyond?

PHILOSOPHY AND GOALS

It is easy to say that the goal of the mentoring program is to help teachers. But to help teachers in what ways? Heller and Sindelar's (1991) work in the field indicate that goals for the mentors might include:

(*1*) To increase the protegé's instructional competence
(*2*) To increase the protegé's self-confidence
(*3*) To be a resource to the protegé in the areas of discipline, classroom management, curriculum, and lesson planning
(*4*) To be a resource to the protegé in the areas of school policy, procedures, and routines
(*5*) To be a friend. (p. 11)

MENTOR ROLE IN EVALUATION

A philosophical issue to be determined early in the planning stages is that of the mentor's role in evaluation of the protegé/new teacher. A nonevaluative role for the mentor makes the program's philosophy one of support, help, and encouragement. A nonevaluative role adds to the likelihood of the new teacher coming to the mentor more frequently with questions and concerns. Would *you* take a lot of questions to your mentor if he/she played a large role in your review for re-employment and tenure? If the district decides that the mentors will play a role in the evaluation of the new teachers, that role must be clearly defined, with the existing state and district evaluation policies considered.

Why would some mentors play a role in evaluation? In some large schools, the administration does not have the time or personnel to adequately observe teachers using a clinical supervision model that includes preconferences, formal observations, and postconferences. A district wishing to implement a more teacher-driven evaluation process may negotiate for the mentors to play a larger role in evaluation. It can be argued that the mentor who is in the classroom on a weekly basis may have a much better idea of the new teacher's effectiveness. In one district, new teachers have the option of one formal visit by the principal with the rest of the evaluative observations completed by the mentor (who was a full-time mentor). Another option is for the mentor to write a letter of recommendation at the end of the first year for the new teacher's file. The letter is done in addition to the formal evaluation completed by the principal/evaluator. Many new teachers ask their mentors for letters of recommendation if they are job searching at the end of one or two years in the district.

CONFIDENTIALITY IN MENTORING

Informal evaluation is tied very closely to the confidentiality issue. It is so easy for an administrator to see the mentor in the hall and ask, "How is our new teacher doing?" Many times principals ask this question of the teacher next door, even if he/she is not the designated mentor! Good evaluation is not hearsay, nor should it be based on what is overheard from veteran teachers about the new teacher. The confidentiality issue should be decided early.

One district with which I worked wanted total confidentiality in the mentor-new teacher relationship so that new teachers would go to their mentors with concerns. Their administrators were trained to expect that if they asked a mentor how a new teacher was doing, the mentor would say, "As you know, I'm the mentor, the keeper of all secrets. I encourage you to visit with and begin your evaluation of the new teacher." The mentors received the same training and the new teachers were given this information in the orientation sessions. I later consulted with another district and gave this example. The administrators in District 2 said that they would never allow a mentoring program to begin if this were the case. For many districts there must be some middle ground on the confidentiality issue; yet that middle ground must be made explicit enough so that all participants understand the parameters of confidentiality.

A district can develop a confidential mentor-new teacher program, with the guidelines that if a new teacher brings a concern to the mentor about the health or welfare of children in the class, then the mentor and the new teacher together must report the concern. (Think about the child abuse report laws already in effect here.) There would have to be a guideline regarding admission of the new teacher about breaking a school code rule or ethical practice rule. I have used the following scenarios in mentor training and administrator academies regarding the confidentiality issue of the mentor-new teacher. Think about and/or discuss these scenarios. How would you react as the mentor? As the school principal?

SCENARIOS

(*1*) The mentor has had a long day at school and runs into the neighborhood pizza parlour to pick up a pizza for her family. While picking up the pizza, she sees her protegé, the new male social studies teacher, at a table with four of the senior baseball players. The teacher has a beer in front of him and there is a pitcher of beer on the table. The students also have half-empty glasses in front of them. What should the mentor do? What are her responsibilities?

(2) A mentor drops by the new teacher's apartment with some homemade soup and a sample of a new test that he feels the new teacher may want to use. When invited into the apartment, the mentor can't help but notice how much computer and video equipment is in the apartment, and several pieces look like those missing from the school. The new teacher says that the media specialist has loaned him some things "long-term." Should the mentor do anything?

(3) The new teacher goes to her mentor and reports that a little girl in her room has told her that her stepfather hits her. The new teacher adds that the little girl says the teacher is not supposed to tell anyone, or

the stepfather may kick her and her mother out of the house. What should the mentor do?

You see from these scenarios that mentoring can become challenging very quickly! That's why the philosophy behind the program and the parameters of the confidentiality issues are so important. One principal succinctly summarized his school's mentoring program when he compared it to someone giving first aid. Someone who administers emergency first aid does so with the best of intentions and knows that there is a point where he/she must stop and wait for more trained medical personnel. A good mentor provides support but recognizes that the new teacher must accept professional responsibilities for himself/herself. The confidentiality issue was well summarized by a mentor who said, "I would treat my new teacher with the same professionalism I treat all my colleagues. If any of my colleagues did something illegal, unethical, or hurtful for students, I would make my conscience my guide in how I dealt with the situation."

PROGRAM LEADERSHIP AND COST

"Who will coordinate/direct the program?" The superintendent, assistant superintendent, principal, assistant principal, staff developers, teachers, and outside consultants may all play roles, but someone must be responsible to make sure that the program runs smoothly. A planning committee consisting of the director and teachers is always a good starting place. In many districts the initiative to start the mentoring program has come from a group of concerned teachers and/or the teachers' organization. Some state affiliates of the National Education Association or of the National Federation of Teachers may have consultants available to speak to the teachers about initiating a mentor program. Including the teachers' association/union from the beginning will help as you later have discussions about teachers serving as voluntary or paid mentors.

The director needs be someone who has time available for the program, secretarial support to help with mailings and arrangements, and knowledge of securing and administering the program budget. Other costs for the program include salary/released time for consultants and teachers who train the mentor teachers, compensation and/or substitutes for the mentors, compensation and/or substitutes for the new teachers (to attend meetings, work with their mentor), snacks, refreshments,

meals for orientation, photocopies, books, videos, and resource materials for both mentors and new teachers, and thank-you/welcome gifts.
One district budgeted money for each mentor-new teacher pair to attend
a professional conference. (This was one incentive to be a mentor, since
non-mentors did not receive this perk.)

WHO WILL MENTOR?

The director and the original planning committee should develop selection criteria for mentor selection. According to Heller and Sindelar
(1991, p. 12), mentors should be:

(*1*) Excellent teachers
(2) Team players
(3) Matched in subject and grade level of their protegé

There can be debate over all criteria, even the three listed above. While
we do want mentors who are role model-quality teachers, does being a
skilled second-grade teacher necessarily make one skilled at helping a
new second-grade teacher get started in the classroom? Some successful
teachers may be so set in their ways of presenting their material that they
fail to recognize that other methods exist! A good mentor is indeed a
good teacher, but one who also knows about the many ways of teaching
and about adult development and teacher education. A good mentor is a
good teacher who respects diversity among students, always strives for
self-improvement, and knows how to create positive classroom climate.
Fawcett (1997) poses the the question, "Is a good teacher always a
good mentor," in her article of that title. She points out that good teachers
know pedagogy and the teaching of children, and that good mentors need
to be versed in the theories of *andragogy*, the teaching of adults. Mentors
must know the tenets of adult learning theory and recognize that their
new teachers need to be self-directed learners. As an adult learner, the
new teacher already has a rich background of experiential knowledge,
which serves as a resource for learning "on the job."
Fawcett further advises that

> Mentors must be careful not to project what they need to know and do onto new
> teachers who are at a different stage in the career cycle. . . . Teachers at the induc-
> tion stage strive for acceptance by students, peers, and supervisors and attempt
> to achieve a comfort and security level in dealing with everyday problems and
> issues. Mentors must be sensitive to these needs and assist the entry year teachers

in dealing with them. The fact that entry year teachers are not concerned with higher level issues of education does not imply that they are any less intellectual or competent. Their needs at this stage in their career are legitimate and must be dealt with before they can move on. (p. 20)

It is critical that those chosen to mentor are team players, or at least are teachers who recognize that teaching should not take place in a vacuum. It is so easy for new teachers to be overwhelmed by the negatives heard in the teachers' lounge. They need mentors who encourage them to get to know and work with their colleagues in a professional manner.

There are definite advantages when a mentor and new teacher share the same subject and grade areas, as they can "talk shop" and share very specific teaching hints with regard to the curriculum. However, it can also be said that "good teaching is simply good teaching" and that any skilled teacher can be a help to a beginning teacher. A third-grade teacher who mentors a teacher of first or second grade can share a lot about what will be expected of the students in the next year. One of my best mentors was a high school business teacher. While she didn't speak a word of Spanish (my subject area), she was a master at helping me learn to organize the room, the students, my gradebook, and so on. She was a tremendous help in working with me to understand the expectations of parents and of the principal.

The mentor needs to be in close proximity to the new teacher. If the mentor is just down the hall, and shares the same preparation time or lunch hour as the new teacher, they will have more opportunities to interact with each other. One advantage for creating a cadre of retired teachers to mentor is that they have more available time and can come into the classrooms as needed.

INFORMING THE FACULTY ABOUT THE MENTORING PROGRAM

The district should disseminate all information about the new program freely. Write a letter (see sample in Figure 3) to all teachers about the establishment of the program, inviting all interested to apply to become a mentor (see application worksheet in Figure 4). State how to apply to be a mentor, listing the applicable criteria and how the decisions will be made. In essence, do an abbreviated version of advertising, recruiting, and selecting mentors as outlined in the earlier chapters of this book for hiring new teachers.

Dear teachers:

Do you remember your first year of teaching? Did you want someone to turn to with all of your questions? Now that you are established in your career, you can help another new teacher "set sail" in the teaching profession by serving as a mentor.

As you know, our district continues to grow and we anticipate hiring seventy new teachers next year. The Teachers' Association Executive Board has worked together with the office of the assistant superintendent for the past two months to develop guidelines to begin a teacher mentor program. We are very excited about implementing a mentor program to help welcome and support our new colleagues. Other districts have experienced great success with programs of teachers mentoring teachers.

Seventy teachers will be named as one-on-one mentors to the new teachers. Those chosen to serve as mentors will be expected to complete three days of training over the summer (choice of June or July sessions) and will be paid for those training days. In addition, the mentors will be paid for three days of work the week before the beginning of the school and will receive a $350 honorarium payment at the mentor banquet in late May.

Our mentor program is nonevaluative in nature, and mentors will not be reporting on the progress of new teachers to the administration. Evaluations of new faculty will continue to be completed by the building principals as in the past.

We need your expertise and experience to support the new faculty in our district. Please read the following application to be a mentor and sign up now! Thank you!

Figure 3 Letter to solicit mentors.

Name:

School and grade/subject:

Years of teaching experience:

Workshops attended, continuing education hours earned, graduate work completed:

Professional memberships, conferences attended:

Training or experience working with education students, student teachers, or other beginning teachers:

Experiences presenting workshops or mentoring other teachers or adults in the community:

I want to serve as a mentor because . . .

One piece of advice that I would share with a new teacher is . . .

Include below the name of one colleague or administrator who would recommend you to be a mentor.

Figure 4 Mentor application worksheet.

CREATING A TRAINED POOL OF MENTORS

Some districts find that it is useful to create a pool of mentors and provide training for thirty teachers to be mentors if they anticipate hiring twenty to twenty-five teachers. The second year that the program is in existence, additional teachers can complete mentor training and those reappointed can take a quick refresher/support course presented in one afternoon. The state of Georgia has created a statewide pool of mentors by offering a course through its regional offices of education and some colleges for an endorsement to a teaching certificate in mentoring new teachers. The state also pays the stipends for the mentoring of new teachers.

When selecting mentors, do not overlook releasing teachers from their classrooms to be full-time mentors for a year or more. I often think that I would have stayed in high school teaching if I could have been a high school teacher in the mornings and a mentor of new teachers in the afternoons.

MENTOR TRAINING

The person or team charged with conducting mentor training must remember first and foremost that they are teaching veteran, experienced teachers. The trainer needs to capitalize on the years of experience and expertise of those in the room. The trainer cannot just lecture! This is a time for active learning and many participatory activities. I like to begin my sessions with introductions where the teachers complete the sentence, "During my first year of teaching I wish someone would have told me . . ." These introductions are then used to build a list of problems of beginning teachers. A good follow-up is to ask teachers what is different now from when they were beginning teachers. There will always be one person who jokingly says, "Well, we don't drive the horse and buggy to school." The list generated by the second question inevitably includes references to technology, the social and emotional problems of today's kids, and the deluge of state-mandated curriculum and testing. Reassure teachers that as they mentor the new teachers regarding these issues, they too will learn a lot. The best mentor training not only prepares the mentor to help the new teacher, but may also serve to regenerate the mentor's attitude and teaching.

Once the problems and concerns of new teachers are outlined, ask the group how they can help the new teacher with those problems. This round of questions will generate the roles and responsibilities involved in the district's mentoring program. The basic issues of time, payment, and resources available should be included in this section. Teachers will quickly answer that their role as mentors is to help the new teacher to be effective in the classroom. At that time, pose the question, "What is effective teaching?" As follow-up questions ask, "What does effective teaching look like?" and "How can we promote effective teaching by the new teachers?"

As the mentors reflect on their own teaching, they can discuss and share effective strategies. Create materials from the list generated for the mentors to use with their new teachers. I often divide the group into groups of three to write their best teaching strategies on poster paper and then share with the group. I turn the papers in to the secretary who then makes a list for the mentors' handbook. Since it is created by the teachers themselves, they are more apt to share these ideas with the new teachers. I always keep overheads with ideas from the literature about effective teaching and handouts from former sessions to "prime the pump" if teachers need some help getting started.

MORE ABOUT MENTOR ROLES

Ganser (1997) analyzed mentor roles from the point of view of both mentors and new teachers. That study summarized important mentor roles to include providing general support and encouragement, helping with curriculum and teaching, explaining logistics and paperwork, discussing "fitting in," and providing help to the new teacher in evaluation of student's work.

The participants in the Ganser study provided evidence that the mentor's role is often ambiguous. The ambiguity arises as mentors ask themselves, "How much should I help when I see a problem?," and as frustrated new teachers ask, "Why isn't my mentor helping me more?" Again, mentor training sessions are the time to address these issues and to create realistic program guidelines.

COLLEGIAL SUPERVISION

One way that effective teaching can be promoted is through collegial supervision of the new teacher by the mentor. This type of supervision is NOT evaluation, but rather a model where the mentor observes the new teacher in order to help him/her reflect upon his/her own teaching. The steps of collegial (also called clinical) supervision include a pre-conference, an observation, and a post-conference. At the pre-conference the mentor and new teacher discuss what the new teacher will be teaching during the observation. Hopefully, the new teacher has also received instruction about the collegial supervision model and begins the cycle of observation by inviting the mentor to observe a class. Mentors receive training to ask, "Tell me about what you will be teaching," "How does this fit into the curriculum?," and "How do you think your students will react to this lesson?" As new teachers explain what they plan to teach, they tend to think aloud and often change and improve a lesson simply by thinking it through more carefully.

The observation should be at a mutually agreed-upon time and place, and it should be decided ahead of time how the mentor will record the activities of the class. Most observers like to script the lesson, noting what happened and what exactly was said in the directions and questions by the teacher. They may also script student responses, noting if students are volunteering and looking for numbers of boys called on versus the number of girls. Sometimes the observer may want to go beyond scripting written notes and make a videotape of the lesson. Either way, the recordings of the lesson will be used for the discussion in the post-conference.

Learning to be a good observer is not an easy task. Graduate schools of education offer semester-long courses in clinical supervision. One way to practice supervision is to use pre-existing videotapes of new or student teachers. Explain to the group what the teacher intends to teach and have each participant write questions they would ask this teacher before the observation. Then, have everyone view the tape. Ask the teachers what they recorded regarding the teaching behaviors. Review these comments and then ask what questions they will ask the teacher in the post-conference and how they will begin the post-conference. It is always amazing to see the reactions of veteran teachers to tapes of beginners. Some may think that a given teacher is hopeless and that there is no way to help him/her become effective. Others will think that the pace of the beginner's lesson is tediously slow. Show samples of good lessons as well, so that teachers may see an effective lesson and discuss how to reinforce the positive lesson. The tapes need to be of teachers who do not work in the district. Professors at nearby universities may be able to supply sample tapes, or tapes can be purchased through professional organizations such as Kappa Delta Pi and Association for Supervision and Curriculum Development. (For more about supervision, see Glickman, 1985.)

After viewing the tape, have one teacher play the role of the mentor and one play the role of the new teacher for the post-conference. Teachers can have fun with this if the designated new teacher reacts emotionally to the mentor's comments. Use a number of tapes so that teachers get some idea of the variety of lessons they may encounter with a new teacher. And yes, let them laugh as they role-play scenarios! This is also a good time to discuss the issues of positive reinforcement of the new teacher. The goal of collegial supervision is to get new teachers to reflect upon their teaching so that they can improve independently. However, many new teachers lack confidence in their abilities and need some positive reinforcement as they strive to improve during their first year. Each mentor must decide how and when praise is appropriate, based upon the needs of the new teacher.

CASE STUDIES

Case studies are also excellent for role-plays during mentor training. The instructor can create them or the veteran teachers can write problem scenarios and then trade their scenarios with each other to solve. Samples can include:

(*1*) Your new teacher is staying at school until 7 or 8 o'clock at night and is still seen carrying bags of materials home to grade. When approached about this, she is defensive and says that this is what it takes to teach the way she wants to teach. What, if anything, do you say to her?

(*2*) During your observation of a new teacher, you see him teach some inaccurate material regarding a complicated science topic. How do you react?

(*3*) The new teacher is doing very well, but confides in you that she is ready to quit, since the job is just too hard and she feels that she is not doing well. In addition, she thinks that the principal does not like her. What would be your approach to this new teacher?

(*4*) Your new teacher reports financial trouble and asks you for a loan. Your response?

(5) The new teacher comes to your room at 3:30 P.M. and reports that she gave detentions according to the school policy to two students who were really acting out. The principal reversed the detentions and sent her a note stating that he didn't think that the students' behavior merited detention, just a little pep talk. The new teacher is obviously concerned. What will you say to this teacher?

(6) When you ask the new teacher how her day went, she replies, "I'm really bummed. One of my students said that another English teacher told him that if he really wanted to learn English this year, he should transfer out of my class. What kind of colleague would tell a student that?" What would your response be to the teacher?

Once the roles of the mentors are established and collegial supervision addressed, the teachers will want resource information about classroom management, discipline, stress management, and the other topics of concern for the beginning teachers. At this point in the mentor training I share the information that I teach in the seminars for beginning teachers. Of course, when the resources are presented to veteran teachers there can be much more discussion of the pros and cons of the writer and much more debate about the practicality of the strategies. For example, when I present Lee Canter or Harry Wong on management, I get much feedback and input from the practicing teachers. I have also found that the mentor teachers often rate this part of the mentor training very highly, as they feel it is a nonthreatening way to update their own skills and knowledge. (For the specific resources for teaching this section of the training, see Chapter 11 about seminars for beginning teachers. Also, if funds permit, purchase one or two books for each mentor or start a mentor library for resource books and materials.)

HOW ADULTS LEARN

Woven into the mentor training should be some of the background about how adults learn, since the new teachers are adults and need to treated as such. (See Fawcett, 1997, and Knowles and Associates, 1984.) In addition, mentors need to understand the developmental stages of all teachers, in order to recognize that what is important to a novice teacher is different from what is of concern to a more experienced teacher. (See Steffy and Wolfe, 1997.)

One good way to end mentor training is for the participating teachers to share their motivation for remaining in the teaching profession. If time permits, have each teacher write about his/her motivation or share a favorite inspirational reading. Most veteran teachers have files of handouts and enjoy sharing articles, poems, and so on.

FOLLOW-UP FOR MENTORS THROUGHOUT THE YEAR

It is often best to provide mentor training in the spring so that mentors can be paired with new teachers as they are hired and mentoring can begin in late summer. As the new school year orientations are scheduled, include time for a half-day "refresher" workshop for the newly assigned mentors. During this workshop they can review what they learned the previous spring and discuss questions and concerns that have occurred to them over the summer. It is good also to review the meeting times, agendas, and all other details of launching the mentor program. Other topics at the session can include more developmental stages of teachers (Steffy and Wolfe, 1997) and mentoring styles (Sweeny, 1994). It is always good to review mentor liability and what to do if the mentor pairing does not work.

If possible, schedule two or three short sessions during the school year for the mentors to meet again. These "support group" sessions can prove very valuable for alleviating mentor stress and improving the program for the next year. Teachers will have much to share about the program. Many find that as they discuss ways to improve the work conditions of the new teachers, they are improving the conditions for all the teachers in the school. The collegiality created within the group of mentors is an added bonus from the process.

PAIRING OF MENTORS AND NEW TEACHERS

As soon as the new teachers are officially hired, the pairing process can begin. Again, the program director can make the pairings. In a district-wide program, the program director may want to share the pairing process with the building principal and/or teacher committee at the building level. Keys to successful pairings include the proximity of mentor to the new teacher, time available for mentoring, and compatibility of the two individuals.

What might result in a difficult pairing? In one school the pairing of a male mentor with a female new teacher proved difficult because some students and faculty thought the two were "just spending two much time alone together over coffee." Obviously, mentoring takes time and spending time over coffee may be a good way to promote discussion, but in today's world these types of problems may occur. A more typical problem is that of veterans who perceive their way of teaching to be the only way and cannot help the new teacher because of their differing perceptions of effective teaching. Some new teachers are equally unwilling to change their teaching—even if it is their first year and what they are doing is not working! The area of mentor pairing is one where more formal research is needed.

PROGRAM EFFECTIVENESS AND
EXTENDED MENTORING

Throughout the school year, send surveys to both the mentors and new teachers to assess the effectiveness of the mentoring program (see Figures 5 and 6). Teachers will be very vocal about the positives and negatives of the program. Include some quantitative statements as well as open-ended questions.

On a scale of 1 to 7, with 1 indicating complete disagreement and 7 indicating complete agreement, rate your agreement with the following statements.

(*1*) My mentor has provided me with practical hints and ideas this year. _____
(*2*) My mentor and I meet on a regular basis. _____
(*3*) My mentor has time to answer questions and listen to my ideas. _____
(*4*) It has been clear to me how my mentor can and cannot assist me. _____
(*5*) My mentor has observed my classes and provided feedback. _____
(*6*) My mentor has helped me to find resource books and materials. _____
(*7*) My mentor and I have problem-solved together. _____
(*8*) My mentor treats me as a colleague. _____
(*9*) I would recommend a mentor pairing for other newly hired teachers. _____
(*10*) My mentor has helped me to improve my teaching this year. _____

A. They most helpful aspects of having a mentor are . . .

B. I would like to see the mentor program improved by . . .

C. Even with a mentor, I still need more information or help with . . .

Figure 5 *Mentor program evaluation (completed by the new teacher).*

On a scale of 1 to 7, with 1 indicating complete disagreement and 7 indicating complete agreement, rate your agreement with the following statements.

(*1*) My new teacher was receptive to practical hints and ideas. _____

(2) My new teacher and I meet on a regular basis. _____

(3) My new teacher asks questions and listens to my ideas. _____

(*4*) It has been clear to the new teacher how I can and cannot assist him/her. _____

(*5*) I observed the new teacher's classes and provided feedback. _____

(*6*) I helped the new teacher to find resource books and materials. _____

(*7*) My new teacher and I have problem-solved together. _____

(*8*) My new teacher and I work as colleagues. _____

(*9*) I would recommend a mentor pairing for other newly hired teachers. _____

(*10*) My new teacher has helped me to improve my teaching this year. _____

A. They most rewarding aspects of being a mentor are . . .

B. I would like to see the mentor program improved by . . .

C. To be a more effective mentor, I still need information or help with . . .

Figure 6 *Mentor program evaluation (completed by the mentor).*

Does the mentoring pair come to an end with the finish of the school year? It can be argued that second-year teachers may be more receptive to professional growth than first-year teachers because the first year is mainly a "survival" year. Once new teachers decide that they can survive, then they can thrive! Once their confidence is built by surviving one year, they may be ready to improve their teaching and deal with more student issues. Hence, the mentor conversation may be even more effective the second year. If it is possible to continue a mentor pairing to the second or third year, by all means do so. In actuality, the mentors will probably continue the dialogue informally now matter the official policy. After all, teachers are teachers.

BENEFITS FOR THE MENTORS

Just as working with a student teacher can help a veteran teacher to rejuvenate and feel more positive about the teaching profession, so too can working with a beginning teacher. Teachers who are selected to serve as mentors feel that their district has recognized and rewarded their expertise. They find that in helping a new teacher to become established, they spend time reflecting upon their own teaching practice and improving upon that practice. Many report that they learn new ideas from their mentees. In Ganser's (1997) study, mentors reported that their work gave them the opportunity to "give something back" to the profession. One mentor said, "I think for the mentor there's the instinct value of knowing that your suffering has spared someone else's suffering, [that] they are not going to have to suffer quite as much as you did" (Ganser, 1997, p. 50).

DISCUSSION QUESTIONS

(*1*) Will the mentors in your district serve in nonevaluative or evaluative roles? Why?

(*2*) You have just been asked to summarize the cost and value of the mentoring program to your local school board. If you must do so in ten minutes or less, what will you say?

(*3*) Local newspapers often seek human interest stories from schools. Would your mentoring program be a good story for the newspaper? Is this a way to seek positive public relations?

(*4*) Discuss ways to further reward the teachers who serve as mentors (stipends, travel, release time).

KEY POINTS

(*1*) The levels of mentoring in a school program may vary widely. Some mentors are volunteers who just answer occasional questions from new teachers. Others observe and work with the new teachers several hours per week. Some veteran teachers mentor as a full-time job.

(*2*) Planning for a mentoring program should begin one year before implementing the program. Budget, personnel, goals, and philosophy are important decisions.

(*3*) Most mentoring programs remain nonevaluative in nature, with the school administration retaining the responsibilities of evaluation.

(*4*) The issue of confidentiality may make the difference in the success of the mentor-new teacher relationship.

(*5*) Mentor training is critical to the success of the program, as is a "good match" of mentor to new teacher, with time available for the two to work together.

CHAPTER 13

Rejuvenating All Faculty

Like so many of the good news–bad news jokes, there is both good and bad news
about educational burnout. The bad news is that educational burnout is fatal—
fatal both in the sense that many very good educators are leaving the educational
profession as a result of being burned out, as well as being fatal in the sense that
people do literally die as a result of physical ailments such as heart attacks and
ulcers caused by the high amount of stress resulting from educational burnout.
The good news about educational burnout is that burnout can be prevented and
cured. (Walter 1988, pp. 105–106)

MUCH HAS BEEN written about the stress of teaching and teacher
burnout. Burnout refers to the emotional exhaustion, depersonalization,
and sense of failure that results from the stress of teaching (Kronowitz,
1992). Kronowitz writes that the sources of the stress are societal, school,
and personal in nature. A *societal stress* might be low salary or constant
bombardment of negative media about the teaching profession. *School
stress* results from too many students in too small a space, the constant
demands of multiple preparations and paper grading, and the strain of
dealing with the many needs of today's students. It *is* stressful to teach six
fifty-five-minute classes a day to over 180 teenagers at the high school
level or to keep over 30 first-graders on task and learning for a whole
day. *Personal stresses* include dealing with financial concerns, one's
own children, aging parents, health concerns, and all of the day-to-day
concerns of just living.

Walter (1988) writes that the first step in preventing burnout is to
identify the symptoms and that prevention occurs when intervention
strategies are identified. Not only do the symptoms and interventions
have to be identified, but the teacher involved must admit the truth to
himself/herself and be willing to use the intervention strategies. As an
example of this, I attended a stress management workshop years ago
where the presenter spent all day teaching us that only we could identify
our stress and that only we could figure out how to cure the stress. Many

people at the workshop could identify the stress and its prevention, but then said that they were unwilling or unable to change their behavior. Does this apply to teachers and the specific stressors of the profession just as it may apply the overall populace?

Induction and mentoring provide help and support to beginning teachers as a means to prevent burnout in the early years of the teacher's career. Induction programs strive to retain promising new teachers—keeping them from "burning" out of the profession early. What supports exist for retaining other teachers in the profession? How can we keep experienced veterans with much-needed expertise in the field? How do we rekindle the boundless enthusiasm that first-year teachers experience?

Steffy and Wolfe (1997) write that teachers make decisions that lead them into growth or withdrawal and "To maintain professional growth, teachers must continually experience or initiate a process of reflection and renewal" (p. 5). They recommend that all educators become aware of the stages of the career and life cycle of teachers, and that professional development efforts encourage reflection, renewal, and growth. Three of their specific recommendations include:

> Administrators support the reflection-renewal-growth cycle by addressing unique needs of teachers operating in different phases.
> Teachers in withdrawal are encouraged to reflect on their profession and instead grow; those who choose not to grow must not be tolerated in the system.
> Teachers entering at the novice and apprentice levels are mentored with the help and support they need to continue to grow into expert teachers. (p. 21)

When do busy teachers find the time for reflection, renewal, and serious professional development? Much reflection can take place by attending a professional conference, even if it is just for one day. Observing in another teacher's classroom can be an invaluable experience. Also, participating in mentor training can present many opportunities for reflection, since working with a student teacher or newly hired teacher causes the mentor to think about his/her own teaching practice. We have all heard the phrase, "You don't really know something until you have to teach it." This phrase has some merit, and in working with new teachers, we are teaching the art and science of teaching.

Even if no opportunities exist for working with new teachers, time can be allotted for veteran teachers to work together and discuss the stressors and burnout factors of teaching. Scheduled inservices, seminars, and workshops can address these issues.

"REJUVENATING AS A TEACHER" SEMINARS

After I had been teaching seminars for new teachers for over four years, I was asked by a group of administrators if I would teach the same material to a group of their veteran teachers, but call the seminar "Rejuvenating as a teacher." The curriculum included organizational strategies, dealing with today's students, classroom management, innovative teaching strategies, and stress management. In developing and teaching this seminar to approximately seventy teachers during a two-year block of time, I gained insight into the needs of veteran teachers, and how the teachers themselves could generate ideas and interventions to prevent their own burnout.

As the "rejuvenating" seminars began I tried to get to know the teachers as well as possible, given the limitations of the one and one-half day workshop format. Quite a lot of time was spent on introductions and the ice-breaking types of activities listed in Chapter 11. At the end of the first half-day I asked the teachers to write a paper describing the challenges, problems, and stresses that they felt in their current teaching positions. Many wrote about the stress caused by dealing constantly with children with social and emotional problems, as well as the stress caused by not being able to raise achievement scores and get all children to learn more. Several veterans wrote about the fact they no longer get to "really teach" because their classrooms had revolving doors and there were simply no blocks of time for teaching. (They meant that children were constantly coming and going to other activities.) They also wrote about dealing with irate parents and administrators who did not understand their teaching situations. Some were very concerned about never being rewarded in the teaching profession. "Not only is there no corporate ladder to climb," one said, "but nobody ever says thank you anymore." Almost all wrote about some type of classroom management and/or discipline problem. They wrote about the stress of dealing with aging parents and/or their own children. None wrote about low salaries, but rather how they felt they had to keep their current jobs to maintain a salary to support themselves and their families. In fact, several wrote that they wished that they could leave but did not see a way out financially if they did so.

The second day of the workshop began with activities for communicating with parents, colleagues, and students; classroom management and discipline; and teaching strategies. Then, after I had time to review the first papers, the teachers read at least one other person's paper and helped that person to write a second paper. In the second paper each teacher was to write one specific goal or change that he/she could implement within the classroom. The papers showed evidence that the material presented was helping teachers to see new ideas and that the ideas shared by other teachers in the workshop would be implemented.

Examples from teachers' papers include the following:

> It was good to discuss the problems because I found out that these problems are universal. Every has similar stressors in the teaching field. I decided to work on the stress that comes from juggling teaching, taking classes, family, and household chores.

> This class has helped me focus on what I need to change. Dealing with a difficult student this year really absorbed all my energy. This was the biggest contributor to burnout. I plan to use the strategies from class to accept and deal with future difficulties.

> My source of frustration that I am going to strive to change is the lack of parenting behind many of my students. Having been a teacher for twenty-eight years, I do realize I am not going to be able to go to my students' homes and convince their parents to suddenly nurture and care for their children. . . . I will not give up on trying to establish some communication with these parents.

The last part of the seminar was devoted entirely to stress management and networking. I used the same materials and approach as for the seminars for beginning teachers. There were many discussion activities. The final assignment was for teachers to write a paper about the advice that they would give themselves regarding the problems they wrote about earlier. Specifically, they were to write about balancing teaching and home life, implementing changes in classroom management, teaching strategies, and communication. The teachers had approximately one month to write this paper before it was due.

The teachers overwhelmingly wrote that simply getting together and talking with other teachers in the workshop helped them to relieve stress! Many said that they would implement informal support groups in their schools. These groups could meet after school and teachers could take turns sharing ideas for teaching. The teachers related that they needed an outlet for "talking about teaching" and for sharing their own expertise. Other teachers wrote that they would strive to identify their stressors and attend future workshops on specific areas of concern (teaching ADD/ADHD children or using computers, for example). Many wrote that they would read some updated books about management and communication. Some wrote about starting a master's program or beginning a personal fitness regime. In essence, these teachers gave themselves very good advice.

Examples from the teachers' final papers include:

> As I begin telling of the advice that I would give myself, I first of all realize that I must take care of myself. I cannot take care of others if I have not taken care of myself. I must remember that I am only one person and that I truly am doing the best that I can do. In fact, as I keep this in mind one of the things that I have changed at school is that I am not afraid to ask others for help in attending to tasks.

> I will continue to read new books on the subject of discipline and inclusion. I will collaborate with our disability and education coordinators. I will seek the advice from other peers. I will see what they have tried and maybe they can observe and have some insights as to where I can improve or change something to make the situation better or tolerable.

> As I approach the half-century mark of my life, I refuse to be left behind and that believe many of my best years in education and my professional development are yet to come. Along with learning new technology, making the leap into graduate school work seems like a giant step . . .

> I have decided to keep a journal now. Not a journal of my inner thoughts, or of my fears and frustrations, but instead a journal of joy. What better way to rejuvenate myself as a teacher than to be able to look back at where I have been and remember why it was I got into this profession in the first place. By sharing the positive aspects of teaching with my fellow teachers as well as my students and family, I believe the results have the power to rejuvenate me.

RETAINING ALL FACULTY

As we look at how to hire the best and the brightest candidates and how to induct newly hired teachers, let's not forget to look at how to keep all faculty "alive and well" in their positions. The complete goal is to find, hire, induct, and keep the best and the brightest in the profession. The teachers themselves are the first people who can provide input about their needs with regard to this area. Are veteran teachers ever asked, "How can the administration and board help you to succeed at your job?" or "What can we do to keep you at our school working with our students?" We need to ask these questions.

Ongoing staff development needs to be collaborative—between teachers, administrators, and colleges of education. The school as a workplace is an area for continual improvement. Class size is an issue, as is physical space in the classroom. Time must be given for workshops and inservice programs—and those programs must be of value. Steffy (1989) wrote that staff development should become human development, so that the district looks at the whole teacher, tailoring learning opportunities to teachers' needs.

As someone who works with student teachers on a daily basis, I remain hopeful. I see bright, energetic, well-trained students excited about going out into the world and becoming teachers. They want to change the world of education and make it a better place. A teacher of the future will have to be a teacher, a social worker, a psychologist, and a magician. It is hoped that they go into schools that embrace their work and support them to do the very best job that they can. Teachers who feel supported and rewarded will find ways to combat their stresses and will rejuvenate not only themselves but others in the profession.

DISCUSSION QUESTIONS

(*1*) In your own teaching/administrative experiences, which staff development programs have been most valuable? Why? Can you replicate those types of experiences?

(*2*) Compare and contrast teacher stress and burnout to that found in other professions. Do any other professions provide effective interventions for stress and burnout?

(*3*) Could your district provide exit interviews for those who are leaving the profession? What could be gained by asking those teachers their reasons for leaving?

(*4*) Some very ineffective, "burned out" teachers may be choosing to stay in your school. What can be done to change their assignments and get them remotivated?

KEY POINTS

(*1*) Stress and burnout in teaching are real, and traditional staff development may not provide answers to preventing some of the best new and veteran teachers from leaving the profession.

(*2*) Induction programs can provide supportive environments to keep promising new teachers in the field. Supportive programs provide a curriculum based on the needs of new teachers, but also provide opportunities for personal help from mentors and for personal growth.

(*3*) Programs can be provided to help all teachers rejuvenate and grow in the teaching profession. Some programs are as simple as after-school support groups with talented, positive moderators.

(*4*) The key to staff development, is human development, and programs that address the needs of teachers at the various stages of their career will be successful.

(*5*) Teachers who assume mentorship roles of new teachers may find those roles very rewarding and rejuvenating.

CHAPTER 14

Action Timeline

WHAT TO DO WHEN?

Many ideas and suggestions have been made throughout this book for hiring and supporting new teachers. When do administrators and personnel directors have the time to implement any of these changes? Some districts are large enough to have sufficient staff to dedicate individuals to hiring and inducting new hires, but most will depend upon the administrators, teachers, and support staff already in place to get the job done. Let's look at a calendar to plan how to begin.

January/February

Hiring: January and February are the quiet months when attention can be given to looking ahead at enrollment patterns, retirements, and teacher changes from building to building.

- Make a best approximation of how many new hires are predicted.
- Plan for who will be out in March to do the recruiting.
- Work on realigning or redefining positions (see Chapter 2).

Induction—existing program:

- Provide information to new teachers about finishing the first semester and making changes to the second semester.
- Provide lots of hands-on practical ideas in seminars—such as make-it and take-it sessions for new bulletin boards or learning centers.
- Small-group support sessions are essential for helping new teachers combat isolation at this time.

Induction—starting a program: The planning for a new induction program begins in the fall, one year before implementation. See September/October for induction—new program, first.

- Finalize negotiations with the teachers' association about the new progam.
- Keep the board informed about plans for the mentoring program and new-teacher seminars.
- Mail out letters to all teachers inviting them to be mentors.
- Begin evaluation of applications for mentors.
- Set the dates for mentor training.

March/April

Hiring:

- Attend as many recruitment fairs as possible.
- Bring strong candidates to your school for interviews.
- Extend contracts to strong candidates, especially those in high-demand fields.

Induction—existing program:

- Provide support seminars on stress management and how to end a school year for new teachers.
- Provide special support for new teachers who will not be re-hired (explain RIF procedures, help with job searches, explain unemployment compensation).
- Have new teachers evaluate seminars.
- Provide a follow-up seminar for current mentors to evaluate their roles as mentors and to prepare for next year's new teachers.
- Support mentors whose new teachers were not rehired.
- Train new mentors to enlarge the pool of veteran teachers who can serve as mentors.

Induction—new program:

- Select mentors and begin mentor training seminars.
- Keep faculty and board informed of training to build strong public relations.
- Make decisions about the fall schedule of realease time for new teachers and mentors.

May/June

Hiring:

- If possible, complete hires of new teachers for fall.
- Get contracts to new hires.
- Begin mailing welcome letters to new hires. Include help for finding housing, childcare, and so on.

Induction—existing program:

- Hold a final celebration breakfast or luncheon for new teachers and mentors.
- Thank mentors in writing with a letter and/or certificates.
- Provide continuing mentors with a schedule of events for welcoming new teachers over the summer.
- Begin the pairings of new teachers to mentors.

Induction—new program:

- Complete training of new mentors.
- Begin pairing newly hired teachers with a mentor.
- Inform mentors and new teachers about dates for back-to-school programs.

July/August

Hiring:

- Fill remaining openings and late resignations.
- Make sure that late hires get "caught up" with information about orientation meetings, as well as special help regarding housing.
- Verify that all paperwork is completed by new hires for insurance, certification, and background checks.

Induction (new and existing programs follow the same timeline here):

- Orientation and new teacher workshops take place (see Chapter 10).
- New teachers and mentors meet and work together in their buildings.

- Provide a fun breakfast or luncheon for a great kickoff to your induction program.
- Ready or not, school begins!!

September/October

Hiring:

- Review the hiring process with board.
- Budget money and personnel for spring recruiting.
- Plan to train new principals and/or teachers who will serve on hiring committees.

Induction—existing program:

- New teachers attend seminars on communicating with parents and classroom management.
- Plan a support session for the mentors to discuss their work with new teachers.
- Do a short evaluation to make sure that mentors are meeting with new teachers.
- Make sure that new teachers are prepared for the first open house, the grading process at the end of the first grading period, Halloween, and/or homecoming.

Induction—new program:

- Discuss need for and philosophy of induction with all administrators, teachers' association representatives, and board.
- Determine roles of mentors in the program.
- Find source of funding for program.
- Name a director for induction/mentoring.
- Work closely with teachers' association before developing program.

November/December

Hiring:

- Continue training of new principals and teachers who will help with hiring process.

Induction—existing program:

- Continue seminars for new teachers. Topics may include dealing with students' social and emotional problems, gifted, special education, and inclusion.
- Have mentors discuss the district's policies about Christmas holidays and getting students ready for the holiday break.

Induction—new program:

- Order books and resources for developing the program.
- Locate speakers for mentor training.

REFERENCES

American Association for Employment in Education. 1997. *1997 Job search handbook for educators*. Evanston, IL: Author.

Anthony, R., and S. Head. 1991. *Interview training packet*. Evanston, IL: Association for School, College, and University Staffing.

Ayers, W. 1993. *To become a teacher*. New York: Teachers College Press.

Butterfield, J. 1993. Unload stress for'94. *USA Weekend*, December 31–January 2.

Canter, L., and M. Canter. 1993. *Succeeding with difficult students*. Santa Monica, CA: Lee Canter and Asscociates.

Canter, L., and M. Canter. 1995. *Behavior management in the middle school classroom*. Santa Monica, CA: Lee Canter and Associates.

Clement, M. C. 1991. *A study of students with community college backgrounds in secondary teacher education*. Doctoral thesis, Unversity of Illinois at Urbana-Champaign.

Clement, M. C. 1996, Spring. A curriculum and resources for beginning teacher programs. *Kappa Delta Pi Record* 32 (3): 87–90.

Clement, M. C. 1997, April. *Beginning teachers' perceptions of their stress, problems, and planned retention in teaching*. Paper presented at the Midwest Association of Teacher Educators Annual Meeting, Urbana, IL.

Colbert, J. A., and D. E. Wolff. 1992. Surviving in urban schools: A collaborative model for a beginning teacher support system. *Journal of Teacher Education* 43 (3): 193–199.

Deems, R. S. 1994. *Interviewing: More than a gut feeling*. West Des Moines, IA: American Media Publishing.

Dollase, R. H. 1992. *Voices of beginning teachers: Visions and realities*. New York: Teachers College Press.

Enz, B. 1997. *Teacher's toolbox: A primer for new professionals*. Dubuque, IA: Kendall/Hunt.

Fawcett, G. 1997. Is a good teacher always a good mentor? *Mentor*. Lincolnshire, IL: Mentoring and Leadership Resource Network of ASCD.

Fuery, C. 1991. *Are you still teaching? A survival guide to keep you sane*. Captiva, FL: Sanibel Sanddollar Publications.

Fuery Ruot, C. F. 1994. *Discipline strategies for the bored, belligerent, and ballistic in your classroom*. Captiva, FL: Sanibel Sanddollar Publications.

Ganser, T. (1997). What are the important mentor roles? *Mentor*. Lincolnshire, IL: Mentoring and Leadership Resource Network of ASCD.

147

Glickman, C. 1985. *Supervision of instruction*. Boston: Allyn and Bacon.

Gordan, S. P. 1991. *How to help beginning teachers succeed*. Alexandria, VA: Association for Supervision and Curriculum Development.

Haberman, M. 1995, June. Selecting 'star' teachers for children and youth in urban poverty. *Phi Delta Kappan* 76 (10): 777–781.

Haberman, M. 1995. *Star teachers of children in poverty*. West Lafayette, IN: Kappa Delta Pi.

Haselkorn, D., and A. Calkins. 1993. *Careers in teaching handbook*. Belmont, MA: Recruiting New Teachers, Inc.

Heller, M. P., and N. W. Sindelar. 1991. *Developing an effective teacher mentor program*. Bloomington, IN: Phi Delta Kappa.

Huling-Austin, L., S. Odell, P. Ishler, R. Kay, and R. Edelfelt. 1989. *Assisting the beginning teacher*. Reston, VA: Association of Teacher Educators.

Huling-Austin, L. 1989a. A synthesis of research on teacher induction programs and practices. In *Teacher induction*, edited by Judy Reinhartz. Washington, DC: National Education Association.

Huling-Austin, L. 1989b. *Assisting the beginning teacher: A training package to prepare mentor teachers*. Austin, TX: Austin Educational Associates.

Hunter, M. 1994. *Enhancing teaching*. New York: Macmillan College Publishing Company.

Knowles, M. S., and Associates. 1984. *Andragogy in action: Applying modern principles of adult learning*. San Francisco, CA: Jossey-Bass.

Krannich, C. R., and R. L. Krannich, R. 1997. *Interview for success*. Manassas Park, VA: Impact Publications.

Kronowitz, E. L. 1992. *Beyond student teaching*. San Bernadino, CA: California State University.

Mager, G. M. 1992. The place of induction in becoming a teacher. In *Teacher induction and mentoring*, edited by G. P. Debolt. Albany, NY: State University of New York Press.

National Commission on Teaching and America's Future. 1996. *What matters most: Teaching for America's future*. New York: Teachers College, Columbia University.

Odell, S. J., and D. P. Ferraro. 1992. Teacher mentoring and teacher retention. *Journal of Teacher Education* 43 (3): 200–204.

Parker, Y. 1989. *The damn good resume guide*. Berkeley, CA: Ten Speed Press.

Rogers, C. 1961. *On becoming a person*. Boston: Houghton-Mifflin.

Routman, R. 1996. *Literacy at the crossroads*. Portsmouth, NH: Heinneman.

Schelske, M. T., and J. Romano. 1994. Coping skills and classroom management training for student teachers. *Teacher Educator* 29 (3, Winter): 21–33.

Steffy, B. E. 1989. *Career stages of classroom teachers*. Lancaster, PA: Technomic.

Steffy, B. E. and M. P. Wolfe. 1997. *The life cycle of the career teacher: maintaining excellence for a lifetime*. West Lafayette, IN: Kappa Delta Pi.

Sweeny, B. 1994. *Promoting the growth of beginning teachers: a mentor training manual*. Wheaton, IL: Barry Sweeny, 26 W. 413 Grand Ave. Wheaton, IL, 60187.

Veenman, S. 1984. Perceived problems of beginning teachers. *Review of Educational Research* 54 (2): 143–178.

Walter, G. 1988. *So where's my apple? Diary of a first-year teacher.* Columbia, SC: South Carolina ETV.

Wilkinson, G. A. 1994. Support for individualizing teacher induction. *Action in Teacher Education* 16 (2, Summer): 52–61.

Winebrenner, S. 1992. *Teaching gifted kids in the regular classroom.* Minneapolis, MN: Free Spirit Publishing.

Winebrenner, S. 1996. *Teaching kids with learning difficulties in the regular classroom.* Minneapolis, MN: Free Spirit Publishing.

Wong, H. K., and R. T. Wong. 1991. *The first days of school: How to be an effective teacher.* Sunnyvale, CA: Harry K. Wong.

Wong, H. K., and R. T. Wong. 1998. *The first days of school: How to be an effective teacher* (2nd ed.). Sunnyvale, CA: Harry K. Wong.

MARY C. CLEMENT was a high school Spanish teacher for eight years before pursuing graduate studies. After receiving a master's degree from Illinois State University and a doctorate from the University of Illinois at Urbana-Champaign, she directed the Beginning Teacher Program at Eastern Illinois University from 1991 to 1997. Much of the research for this book came from her programs for new teachers, mentor teachers, and administrators in east-central Illinois. Since 1997 she has been an assistant professor and graduate faculty member at Berry College in Mt. Berry, Georgia, where she also served two years as the director of Field Experiences and Student Teaching.

Clement is also the author of *Put Your Oxygen Mask on First . . . and Other Strategies for Succeeding in Teaching* and *Bright Ideas: A Pocket Mentor for Beginning Teachers*.